Helping Children Cope with the Loss of a Loved One

A Guide for Grownups

WILLIAM C. KROEN, PH.D.

EDITED BY PAMELA ESPELAND

Free Spirit ®
PUBLISHING

The stories in this book are based on actual case studies, but the names have been changed.

Library of Congress Cataloging-in-Publication Data
Helping children cope with the loss of a loved one: a guide for grownups / William C. Kroen; edited by Pamela Espeland.
    p.   cm.
Includes bibliographical references and index.
ISBN 1-57542-000-7 (pbk.: alk. paper)
    1. Bereavement in children. 2. Bereavement in adolescence. 3. Grief in children. 4. Grief in adolescence. 5. Children and death. 6. Teenagers and death. 7. Children—Counseling of. 8. Teenagers—Counseling of. I. Espeland, Pamela, 1951–   II. Title.
BF723.G75K76   1996
155.9'37'083—dc20   95-42431
                                                              CIP

Cover and book design by MacLean & Tuminelly
Index compiled by Eileen Quam and Theresa Wolner

10 9 8 7 6 5 4 3 2 1
Printed in the United States of America

The author gratefully acknowledges the work of Dr. Elisabeth Kübler-Ross, whose descriptions of how preadolescents and adolescents grieve (as set forth in her book *On Death and Dying*) inspired some of the guidelines presented here.

Free Spirit Publishing Inc.
400 First Avenue North, Suite 616
Minneapolis, MN 55401-1730
(612) 338-2068

Dedication

To the memory of my mother and father, Eleanor and William,
and to the memory of my mother-in-law, Katherine Coady Boyle.

Acknowledgments

I would like to thank Maria Trozzi of The Good Grief Program
for her kind assistance.

Contents

Foreword

Dr. William Kroen's book, *Helping Children Cope with the Loss of a Loved One*, is a marvelous primer for parents, teachers, and anyone who is dealing with a bereaved child. In very simple language, Kroen assists us in understanding what a child from infancy through age 18 knows and feels when faced with the death of a loved one. Parents particularly will enjoy the straightforward approach, with no hint of "psychobabble" that can confuse issues for the layperson.

This book is rich in anecdotes that further clarify the child's need to understand, grieve, commemorate, and go on, as specified in the work of The Good Grief Program founder, Dr. Sandra Fox. Kroen weaves together case studies and content with integrity and sensitivity. This book is a wonderful resource for the parent in all of us.

Maria D. Trozzi
Director of The Good Grief Program
Judge Baker Children's Center
Boston, Massachusetts

Introduction

WHO WANTS TO TALK to a child about death? The answer must surely be . . . no one. As adults, and especially as parents, we want to protect our children from painful experiences, and the death of a loved one is the most painful of all. We want to see our children filled with joy, laughing, playing, and learning. We want them to be happy. Although most of us can easily and enthusiastically speak to our children about the mysteries and miracles of life, when it comes to death, we don't have the will—or the words.

But children are people *experiencing* life, not just getting ready for it. Because death is part of life, it inevitably touches them. To be able to understand death, to pass through the stages of grieving in a healthy way, and to carry on effectively are essential to a child's well-being. To be able to grieve appropriately and cope with loss before, during, and after a death enables a child to grow up free of guilt, depression, anger, and fear. When we can help our children heal the pain of the deepest emotional wound—the death of a loved one—we are giving them important skills and understandings that will serve them the rest of their lives.

The childhood years are tender ones, and children should be taught about death tenderly. In an ideal world, we adults would be strong and sensitive and totally focused on them at such a time. The harsh reality is that *their* loved one is often *our* loved one. If you have lost a spouse, a partner, a parent, another child, or someone else dear to you, you may feel completely unequipped to deal with a surviving child's emotional needs. You may be overwhelmed by your own shock, sadness, and sense of bereavement.

1

How can you possibly find the strength to help someone else, especially a child, understand what has happened and how to cope? It is my wish that this book will provide at least some of the answers.

There are no magic formulas for overcoming grief quickly and painlessly. Rather, we must draw on what we have learned from research, scientific study, tradition, and observation, then add a healthy dose of common sense. This book reflects the knowledge, wisdom, compassion, and experience of social scientists, professional caregivers, parents, and other adults who have given careful thought to helping children grieve and have worked closely with grieving children. It owes a great debt to the special people at The Good Grief Program of the Judge Baker Center of Children's Hospital in Boston, Massachusetts. Founded by Dr. Sandra Fox in 1983, this program is nationally recognized for its outstanding work and frequently serves as a resource in crisis situations. In preparing this book, I have turned often to Dr. Fox's work, *Good Grief: Helping Groups of Children Deal with Loss When a Friend Dies* (Boston: New England Association for the Education of Young Children, 1988). I am grateful for the support The Good Grief Program has given me at every step of this process.

Helping Children Cope with the Loss of a Loved One is a guide for parents, teachers, counselors, and other adults who play important roles in children's lives. You may be reading this book because you work with children and you want to be prepared in case death ever touches them. You may be reading it because someone you know is dying and a child will be affected. Or you may be reading it because you are already walking the path of grief. I sincerely hope that you will find comfort and compassion here, along with sound information and practical advice that will help you to help a child . . . and yourself. You are carrying a terrible burden. Others have carried a similar burden; you will meet them here and learn from them. As you will discover, talking about death and grief is an essential step toward emerging as an emotionally healthy human being.

William C. Kroen, Ph.D.
Belmont, Massachusetts

Quick answers to
common questions

IF SOMEONE YOU KNOW and love has just died—a spouse, a parent, a child, a friend—you may not have either the time or the energy to read an entire book. But if children have also been touched by the death, there are things you need to know right away to help them through the initial shock. Following are ten of the most common questions parents ask when a loved one dies, along with brief answers. Read this section first, then return to the rest of the book as soon as you can.

"How can I tell my children about the death?"
Gently and lovingly, using simple, honest words. Sit down with them some-place quiet, hold them in your arms, and tell them. Don't be afraid to say "died" or "dead." For example, you might say: "Something very, very sad has happened. Daddy has died. He will not be with us anymore because he has stopped living. We loved him very much, and we know he loved us, too. We are going to miss him very, very much."

In a few short sentences, tell them how the loved one died. For example: "You know that Daddy has been very, very, very, very sick for a long time. His sickness has made him die." Or: "Daddy was in an accident. He was hurt very, very, very, very badly. The accident made him die." Multiple "very's" help children to distinguish between the loved one's death and the times when they were "very sick" or "very hurt."

Avoid euphemisms for death like "lost," "taken away," "passed away," or "gone on a long journey." They feed children's fears of being abandoned, and they create anxiety and confusion. Never say that a loved one has "gone to sleep." This might make children afraid to go to bed at night.

Many children ask, "What does 'died' mean?" Again, use simple, honest words: "It means that the body has *totally* stopped. It can't walk, breathe, eat, sleep, talk, hear, or feel anymore."

"What can I say when my children ask 'why'?"

"Why did Mommy die?" "Why did Daddy die?" "Why did Grandma have the accident?" "Why did this happen to me?" These are hard questions to answer. It's okay to admit that you've asked the same questions yourself. Then explain that death is part of life for all living things on earth. It happens to everyone. There are things we can control and things we can't control. Death is one of the things we can't control.

Be sure to tell them that no one is to blame for the death—not the loved one who died, not God, and certainly not the children. Say very clearly, "It is not your fault." Nothing they said, did, or thought caused the death.

"Should I talk about the death in religious terms?"

This is a decision each family must make for itself. Generally speaking, it depends on how much religious education your children have. If they have been raised in a faith community, they will be better able to understand your religious references. If they haven't, this is probably not the best time to introduce religion, because they will find it confusing. In any event, avoid saying things like "God took Daddy" or "God wanted Mommy," which may create fear in young children.

"Should my children attend the wake, funeral, and burial?"

This, too, is a decision each family must make for itself. As a general guideline, children six years old and up should be allowed to attend *if they want to.* Joining family members and friends for these important rituals gives children a chance to express their grief, gain strength and support from others, and say good-bye to the loved one. They feel part of a group that is continuing on despite the loss, and they draw comfort and security from being included.

Be sure to prepare them ahead of time by explaining what will happen and what they will see, hear, and do. Tell them whether the casket will be open or closed. Explain that many people will probably be crying. Let them ask questions. If you are too distressed to do this yourself, ask a family member or friend to step in.

What if children don't want to attend these rituals? Don't force them, and don't make them feel guilty for not going.

"Will it harm my children if they see me cry and grieve?"

Not at all. Children need to learn how to express grief, and the best way to learn is from adults who care about them. When you cry, this teaches your children that it's okay to cry. When you look sad, this gives them permission to show their emotions. Of course, if adults keep a "stiff upper lip" and deny their feelings, this is what their children will learn to do, and it is not a healthy response to grief. Don't be afraid to show your emotions in front of your children.

"What if I'm too overcome by grief to attend to my children's needs?"

Before you can take care of your children, you need to take care of yourself. Rest, eat well, and seek comfort and assistance from family members and friends. See if another adult can take over for you until you're ready to help your children.

"Should I tell my children's teachers about the death?"

Yes, and as soon as possible. Teachers can help by monitoring children's behavior and emotional condition in the weeks and months following the death. They can offer guidance and understanding to children who are sad, angry, and upset.

If the school has a counselor (or psychologist) on staff, either full-time or part-time, you should tell him or her about the death as well. Counselors are usually trained to deal with trauma and grief. They can monitor children to make sure that grief and mourning aren't interfering with their learning and development. Counselors are also good sources of information and advice for parents, and they can make referrals to support groups.

"What are some of the ways my children might react to the death, and how should I respond?"

Some children feel guilty or responsible for a loved one's death. They may believe that their angry words or thoughts caused the death, or that their "bad" behaviors caused the death. Reassure them that this is *not* true.

In cases when a parent has died, some children cling to the surviving parent. They become very concerned that he or she will also die and no one will be left to take care of them. This fear of abandonment is perfectly normal. Reassure them that there will *always* be someone to take care of them.

Some children regress into younger behaviors, act out, and throw tantrums. Be patient! You are all under a terrible strain, and your children are less equipped to deal with it than you are. Call attention to inappropriate behaviors, and set and enforce limits as usual.

"When is it okay for my children to start playing again?"

As soon as they feel like playing. Children tend to grieve in spurts. One moment, they'll be crying out of sadness; the next, they'll be laughing as they play on the swings. Play is therapeutic for children. It gives them a break from grieving, offers·them the chance to express their feelings in their own way, and allows them to relieve anxiety and stress through movement.

"What are the most important things I can do for my children right now?"

Be there for them, be honest with them, and love them.

Understanding death

MANY PARENTS TRY to shield their children from learning about death. Yet most children have an awareness of death and are exposed to it daily. Some experts believe that by the time a child reaches the age of 18, he or she will have witnessed nearly 18,000 "deaths," from the fictional deaths portrayed in cartoons, movies, books, comics, and TV programs, to the real but impersonal deaths shown on news broadcasts, to the very personal deaths of peers and family members. When children see a dead bird or squirrel on the street, they are presented with the reality of death. Trying to protect them from it is futile.

Children should be given the chance to learn about death from observations and events in their everyday lives. Parents should seize opportunities to teach their children basic concepts of death and grieving as they present themselves from one day to the next. Finding a dead bird or flower, or experiencing the death of a pet, are perfect times for parents to share their insights on life and death and invite their children to tell them what they are thinking and feeling.

When children learn about death and grieving in a matter-of-fact, sensitive way, they develop good coping skills for facing real crises later on. Especially when there is a death in the family, parents must be up-front with their children. Family secrets don't last long in most families. Obscuring the facts and consequences of a death in the family doesn't really "protect" young children; it only makes them more fearful and anxious.

How did you learn about death?

W HEN IT COMES TIME to teach children about death, most adults draw from their own childhood experiences. If your family tried to hide the concept of death or shield you from the pain associated with it, you will likely use a similar approach with your own children. This way of dealing with death is not wrong, nor is it in any way emotionally abusive. It is not, however, emotionally *helpful*. It does not prepare children for the very real eventuality of death.

Before you can begin to explain death to your children, you may want to start by examining your own childhood experiences. Ask yourself these questions:

- Were you aware of any family secrets about death?

- Did you attend wakes, funerals, or memorials for any family members?

- Did anyone ever talk with you about death?

- Did a family pet die when you were a child? If so, how was the death explained to you?

- Did you have questions about death that you never asked?

- Do you remember what you were told happens when someone dies?

- Did you ever experience a painful loss or separation as a child?

Your answers may give you some insights into how your children currently perceive death. Many parents, in wanting to protect their children, make the subject of death off-limits. They convey their own denial of death to their children. In extreme cases, such denial can lead to emotional detachment among family members, preventing them from being close to each other.

Families who share their feelings develop a sense of closeness and mutual caring. Telling your children that you sometimes feel angry, hurt, sad, confused, and uncertain is a positive, healthy way to let them know it's okay for *everyone* to share powerful emotions. Your children will feel comfortable approaching you on serious subjects, including death.

Accepting death as part of life greatly reduces the negatives associated with this inevitability. Children who learn about death and grieving while they are growing up are better able to handle it when it occurs, without developing false and ineffective methods of coping.

When speaking about death and grieving to your children, truth and honesty are always the best approaches. Being truthful and honest is not the same as being blunt and insensitive. You can talk about death and grieving in a warm, caring, sensitive way. This important aspect of parental love helps your children build skills and abilities to function better in all of life's situations.

How children understand death

CHILDREN PERCEIVE AND REACT to death in many different ways. A child's personality, sensitivity, coping skills, level of development, and abstract thinking skills are just some of the variables that come into play.

Numerous studies indicate that young children perceive and react to the concept of death both *specifically* and *literally*.

- *Specific perception* means that children view death as a specific incident. The death itself, and the concept of death, is focused on the person or animal who has died. The child doesn't think of the death in an abstract or global manner; it is confined to the *one* person or *one* animal of particular importance to the child.

- *Literal perception* means that children take all references to death seriously, including words, experiences, and visual images. A parent's casual comment, "I died laughing," may be no laughing matter to a young child. "You're going to be the death of me" is not a figure of speech but a frightening possibility.

Children usually will not address death, or their concern about the impending death of someone close to them, in a direct manner. They may, however, express their anxiety in a *thematic* manner. For example, a young child whose grandfather is terminally ill may voice her concern that her dog is getting old and might die soon. Often children ask "what if . . ." questions containing anxieties about who will take care of them—or what changes might take place in their lives—without making a specific reference to a particular death or impending loss. They feel upset and worried without knowing why.

Although many young children don't understand death, they are still curious and eager to learn about it. Children easily pick up on their parents' feelings and emotions. They know when a parent is anxious and concerned. They want to be informed and reassured. Because they are in a learning mode, they want and expect to learn.

Studies have shown that children think about, wonder about, and discuss death differently at all stages of their development. Many adults dismiss children's curiosity about death, believing that "they're too young to understand." In fact, death has a significant impact on children of *all* ages, from infancy through adolescence.

Following is a very basic overview of children's perceptions and reactions to death, based on what we know so far and organized by age groups. You will also find suggestions on what you can do for and say to children at each developmental stage.

Infants ages newborn to 10 months*

An infant's mother is usually his or her primary connection to the outside world. While infants cannot specifically identify and discern a particular person as their mother until they are almost a year old, they are adept at recognizing her touch, warmth, scent, and manner as she attends to their needs. She is their main link to life and their most important source of comfort, security, and stability. There is a bond between them.

It is generally believed that infants perceive a mother's death as an "absence." Infants function in the present. A mother's death is a sudden change. The bond is broken. Infants may feel discomfort as they sense the loss of their mother and find new faces and voices in their environment. They may express their discomfort in behaviors including changes in eating and/or sleeping patterns, constant crying, crying for no apparent reason, and irritability.

---

* 10 months or whenever the child begins to use and understand language.

The death of a sibling, father, or other family member may not be as traumatic to an infant as the death of the mother. However, infants will perceive the mother's grief and react to it. A death in the family will interrupt the nurturing routines they are accustomed to. Feeding schedules may change; the mother may be absent for long periods of time; her touch and tone of voice may change. While infants may not be able to comprehend the meaning of what is happening around them, they *will* perceive changes and negative stimuli in their environment.

❧   WHAT YOU CAN DO   ❧

Try to keep the infant's care routine on schedule. Try to minimize unusual sounds and events near the infant—crying, loud voices, large numbers of unfamiliar people—until the environment in the home has returned as much as possible to the way it was before the death. What infants need most during this time is for things to stay as normal as you can make them.

Babies ages 10 months to 2 years

Many babies have the ability to display fear, rage, love, anger, and jealousy as early as 10 months of age. They clearly recognize the adults in their life and know how to interact with them. They are able to sense other people's moods and emotions.

As they move toward their second year, they experience major growth in the areas of memory, language, and socialization. Language holds special meaning and appeal for them; they love to hear familiar voices repeating familiar words and phrases. They are becoming more independent and beginning to recognize that they are individuals.

Babies in this age group are not yet equipped to conceptualize death or understand it. They will experience the death of their mother as a severe loss, since she is usually the person they are closest to and most attached to, but they may not be very profoundly affected by the death of other close family members.

For babies ages 10 months through 18 months, as for infants, it's important to keep household and care routines and schedules as close to normal as possible. Feeding times, play times, storytelling times, singing, and holding should continue without interruption. Stay close to the children and shield them from too much contact with strange faces, voices, sounds, and scents.

Babies ages 18 months through 2 years can understand words and use them to express their feelings. Repeating simple sentences—"Daddy gone," "Mommy no more"—may help them to comprehend that a loss has taken place, and that this is the reason for the upheaval in the home.

Children ages 2 to 5

As children move up the developmental ladder, their concepts and perceptions of the world around them undergo profound changes. Children in this age group tend to be egocentric, extremely curious, and very literal in how they interpret their world.

This is important for adults to understand, especially when trying to teach children the concepts of life and death. Anything you say is likely to be taken as *very* real by your two-to-five-year-old. Base your explanations on fact and reality. Vague explanations or indirect language will create confusion and possibly increase your child's anxiety and fear.

The concept of death for the two-to-five-year-old is very different from that of the adult or even the older child. Children in this age group perceive death as a temporary state. They may equate death with a form of sleeping. In their mind, the dead person still eats, breathes, and exists, and will awaken at some point and return to a full life.

❧ WHAT YOU CAN DO AND SAY ❧

Define death to these children as the fact that the body has *totally* stopped. Explain that a person or animal who is dead can't walk, breathe, or feel anymore. Clearly and specifically state that death is *not* a form of sleeping; the body will *not* wake up. Emphasize the word "totally" to eliminate misconceptions about the state of death. This also helps children who might be confused about death because they have seen (in real life, on TV, or in movies) people who are paralyzed, comatose, or severely disabled—or cartoon characters who always bounce back no matter what happens to them.

Encourage the children to ask questions and partake in family discussions. Put your answers in words that are meaningful to them. For example, children who see a dead bird or pet might ask if people die, too. (Underneath this question may be a concern for their own mortality or the potential death of their parents.) Tell them that people or animals usually die "when they are very, very, very, very old." Using multiple "very's" implies that most humans have a long life and live to an old age. Saying that people or animals usually die "when they are old"—without the "very's"—may be misleading. For preschoolers, a teenager is "old" and their parents and teachers are "very old."

When a death follows an illness, use the multiple "very's" again: "Sometimes people die when they get very, very, very, very sick." This is especially important for children who have had colds, earaches, or the flu, or those who have seen their parents or siblings come down with similar mild illnesses. You might say, "There are many different levels of sickness, and death only happens to people who are very, very, very, very sick with diseases that very few people get."

A good way to assess children's understanding during these learning opportunities is simply to ask, "What do *you* think?" How they respond reflects how well they have grasped the information and gives you the opportunity to fill in any gaps. You don't need to go into extensive anatomical or metaphysical explanations of death for young children. Your goal is to equip them with enough practical and factual knowledge to understand what death is, how and when it happens, and how we should react when it does.

Sharing emotions with young children is healthier than hiding them. At the loss of a beloved pet, it's okay to cry with your children instead of pretending to be above the pain. From this, they will learn that crying and showing deep sadness are normal, natural ways to express strong feelings. Talking about emotions is not a sign of weakness or vulnerability; being honest about how we feel helps us to feel better. Tell your children how you feel and why you are sad and upset over the loss.

Don't reserve this lesson in emotional expression for situations involving death. As much as possible, share how you feel in *all* situations. Letting children know when you feel angry, sad, happy, frustrated, or excited helps them to face and sort out their own feelings.

∽

Death can be confusing

It's important to understand that the words and rituals surrounding death can be very confusing for young children. Examples:

* A wake might seem like a part of death where the dead person is supposed to "wake up"—more "evidence" that death is temporary. Or children might hear the word "wake" and understand it as "wait," meaning that if they wait patiently, the deceased will return.

* The terms "passed away," "expired," and "stopped living" are vague and misleading. Young children don't understand them. They are softer than saying "died," but they are not helpful or meaningful.

* If a loved one dies in a hospital or hospice, children may decide that these are places where people go to die. They may become fearful if they ever need to go to the hospital for any reason. Explain that these are places where everyone tries to help and save the person, but sometimes all of the help doesn't work because the person was "very, very, very, very sick" or "very, very, very, very old."

* Children may perceive funerals and religious services as fitting the explanation that "God wanted Daddy." They may believe that the funeral or service is the time when the person is formally "taken to heaven."

* Children who see the deceased in a coffin may think that the person is sleeping. Be sure to explain that this is not so.

* Children who observe the burial of a loved one without explanation may develop the fear of being buried alive—a fairly common fear among young children (and quite a few adults).

∽

Children ages 6 to 9

By the time children reach the middle years, they have made significant cognitive and developmental leaps. They are much more socially involved, both within the family and with the outside world. They are aware of their role as a family member, a student in school, a friend, and a member of groups. They are able to grasp concepts, value the need to control their behavior, recognize and evaluate what is good or bad, and form opinions.

Although six-year-olds perceive death quite differently from nine-year-olds (whose concept is very close to that of an adult), they share the basic ability to conceptualize the *fact* of death. There are two major developmental changes that make this age group unique. First, six-to-nine-year-olds generally know the difference between fantasy and reality. Second, they can experience guilt.

Children this age have a much greater ability to understand death and its consequences than younger children do. Although they may cling to some of their fantasies, they are able to grasp the reality and, more importantly, the finality of death. However, this does not mean that they are ready to *accept* death or respond to it rationally. The death of a loved one is a trauma that sorely tests their ability to cope.

Following are some of the thoughts children ages six to nine might have when confronted with the death of a loved one.

"Death is forever."

Unlike preschoolers, six-to-nine-year-olds no longer view death as temporary. They know that death is not a form of sleep and that the deceased will not return. On the surface, this level of understanding appears healthy and productive. However, just because they *understand* death doesn't mean they can cope with it.

"If death can happen to someone I know, it can happen to other people I know."

This awareness is a two-edged sword. Although children this age can comprehend that death happens to everyone at some time—that it is part of life—the idea is deeply troubling. A child who loses a parent might fear the loss of the surviving parent. The fear of abandonment is one of the most prominent and pervasive fears found in young children, and the death of a parent feeds directly into this fear.

"If death can happen to someone I know, it can happen to me."
Because of their greater understanding of death, six-to-nine-year-olds may fear that they will die soon. Sometimes they are able to cope by creating a framework of rules or guidelines to "protect" themselves from death. They become more aware of potential dangers and the need to be safety-conscious. They know not to run into traffic, not to be out alone at night, not to talk to strangers, not to jump from high places, not to play with fire.

These basic precautions offer some comfort and reassurance that they can, in fact, shield themselves from death. Children may not articulate this feeling or even be aware of it on a conscious level, but it is present in their approach to daily life.

"Death means change."
A death in the family—even the death of a pet—changes the family dynamic. Children tend to focus on how this change will affect them. They fear that their peers will perceive them as "different." They worry about how their friends and classmates will treat them. They want to be "one of the group," not singled out because someone has died. They wonder if they will have to change schools, change friends, or leave the family home.

"Death means new feelings."
Depression, sadness, anger, guilt, longing, fear, and confusion are some of the feelings children this age may experience. These feelings may be new and unfamiliar, and they will certainly be uncomfortable. If they happen simultaneously, children can be overwhelmed. In an effort to soften and eliminate these feelings, children may ignore them or bury them deep inside.

✺ WHAT YOU CAN DO AND SAY ✺

Be open and honest when talking to children this age about death. Explain the circumstances that caused the death in a sensitive but factual way. Six-to-nine-year-olds want and need to know what happened to make someone die. You might also relate the death to their past experiences with nature—the dead squirrel in the street that was hit by a car, the family pet that died of illness or old age.

Be especially alert to their emotional reactions. Find time to quietly speak with them about their fears and worries. Focus on listening rather than advising or lecturing, since this will give you valuable insights into their emotional state. Let them speak freely—in a safe place, without interruptions—about the death of the loved one or about death in general. Don't be surprised if one, many, or all of the following happen during the course of your conversations:

- Children may repeat the same statements or questions.

- They may start some sentences with "If only . . . ."

- They may blame themselves for contributing to the death.

- They may seek reassurances about the future.

- They may ask what is happening to the dead person's body.

- They may pose questions related to religious and cultural beliefs.

- They may ask about the health and well-being of other family members.

- They may wonder aloud about their own mortality.

- They may ask what will happen to them if someone else dies.

- They may want to know how their role in the family has changed because of the death.

- They may express concerns about school or a lack of interest in school.

- They may worry about what their friends and classmates will think and how they will act.

Be prepared to answer children's questions and address their concerns in a factual and comforting way. Provide them with as much stability, security, and consistency as possible. As children begin to feel safer and more comfortable talking about the death, you will find that their fears, anxieties, sadness, and confusion will gradually diminish.

Religious and cultural beliefs can be comforting

Personal religious or cultural beliefs can be comforting to people in distress, including children. When talking with young children about God or a higher spiritual being, present these concepts in a positive, non-threatening manner. This will help to soothe their fears and ease the trauma of death's finality. You might preface these concepts with "We believe . . . ," then go on to explain how your religion or culture views death. Especially when talking with young children, it is best to avoid topics including hell, purgatory, or judgments of being "good" or "bad."

NATHAN'S STORY

Nathan was a seven-year-old who had been diagnosed with leukemia at age four. Following his diagnosis, he received treatment at a children's hospital for almost two years. His treatment included inpatient stays for chemotherapy, during which he met many other children who were also undergoing chemotherapy. He made friends with some of them and saw them outside the hospital as well as in a hospital play group. Over time, several of his playmates died.

By the time he was six, Nathan's disease had gone into remission, and his prognosis for a full recovery was excellent. His parents told him that the doctors felt his leukemia was leaving his body and he no longer needed chemotherapy. To their surprise, Nathan's response was not one of elation or even relief. Instead, he began to repeatedly ask his mother, "Mommy, am I going to die?" Because his friends had died, Nathan couldn't accept the idea that he was going to live.

Deeply concerned, Nathan's mother sought advice from a therapist. The therapist emphasized that it was important to alleviate Nathan's fears for two reasons. First, the stress from his anxiety could have a negative impact on his immune system, impeding his recovery. Second, his fears could hinder his development in other areas of his life.

The children's hospital had a staff psychiatrist who led a support group for survivors like Nathan. The focus of the group was to reduce the children's anxiety, fear, and guilt. Nathan was able to share his thoughts and concerns with other children and bond with them. He made new friends within the group and grew comfortable with the fact that he was a survivor.

❧

Preadolescents ages 10 to 12

Moving up the developmental ladder, we come to preadolescent children, whose concept of death approaches that of an adult. Clearly, children in this age group will react very differently to death than younger children.

Preadolescents know that death is permanent. They are able to grasp the significance of rituals, understand how the death occurred, and realize the impact death has on them and their family. They may still have questions regarding religious and cultural beliefs, depending on how they were brought up, and they may want to know more about heaven, hell, and life after death. Their comprehension of the future is much more developed than when they were younger, and they think in terms of how a loved one's death will transform their life. On the other hand, some preadolescents may deny that the death has changed their lives. They may insist that they "don't feel anything" or "don't care," then exhibit uncharacteristic anger or even violent behavior.

Preadolescents also have a much stronger sense of their own mortality. Studies have shown that they think about their own death, but they often block out or displace those thoughts to avoid having to deal with them.

✿   WHAT YOU CAN DO AND SAY   ✿

Be available to spend quiet times one-on-one with your preadolescents. Give them the chance to express their feelings without putting their egos at risk. This may mean leaving them alone with their thoughts—and with pictures, music, or other belongings of the deceased loved one. Afterward, offer opportunities for discussion.

Explain that even though the family has changed, you are still there to take care of them. Invite them to share their concerns about the future, and offer reassurances. Answer their questions as openly and honestly as you can, giving specific details when appropriate.

For preadolescents in denial, offer matter-of-fact statements about how life will be different without the loved one, along with examples of how it will stay the same. Whenever possible, assume the role and duties of the deceased, or see if another close relative is able to step in—if the preadolescent will accept this. Explain that this is in no way a "replacement" for the lost loved one, but a continuation of life.

Don't ignore or tolerate excessive anger, acting out, or violent behavior. Seek professional help. This is another way to clearly show that you are present, committed, and concerned.

Adolescents

Adolescents are on the brink of becoming fully developed young men or women, ready to enter the "real world" and begin their lives as adults. They are able to think abstractly and reason, and they are aware of their personal values, strengths, and weaknesses. They have a sense of themselves and their place in society. Death represents the *complete* opposite of everything that is important to them at this point in their lives.

Their understanding of death is comparable to an adult's, but their emotional state is one of constant turmoil and change. On the one hand, because they embrace life so fully—and because they are convinced of their own immortality and omnipotence—it is difficult for them to accept death. On the other, the trauma of death is likely to send them deeper into emotional turmoil. Their reactions may vary widely and change abruptly, from fear to anger, shock, guilt, denial, and regression to childlike thinking.

Death intensifies the pressure they are already feeling as they face the future and its many unknowns. Their first response may be to wonder, "How will this affect *me*, my life, my plans?" They are not being self-centered. They are just being teenagers.

Like preadolescents, adolescents struggle with the awareness of their own mortality. Many have already had some experience with death—perhaps the loss of a grandparent—and they can remember their pain and sadness. Some may drift into a depressed state, withdrawing from friends and family members, isolating themselves, and spiraling down into their own dark thoughts. They may become unusually quiet and spend a great deal of time alone in their rooms or sleeping.

❧ WHAT YOU CAN DO AND SAY ❧

Take a few moments to remember how you felt when you were a teenager. This will put you back in touch with the intense and conflicting emotions of adolescence. Now try to imagine how you might have felt if a loved one had died during that time in your life. No wonder your teenagers are acting so strangely!

If they ask about the causes and circumstances of the death, answer them frankly. Talk with them about how the death will affect them personally. They need to know that you will be truthful with them and that they can trust you. If the death will have a significant financial effect on the family, they will need to know this, too, although you may want to save discussion of the details until later.

Give them the opportunity to participate in all of the ceremonies, rituals, and gatherings involved with the death, and invite them to share in the planning and decision making. On the other hand, be sure to leave time for them to spend with their friends. A quick return to the peer group is essential for adolescents who are feeling "different" because of the death. Encourage them to maintain their regular patterns of eating, sleeping, and socializing as much as possible, and to return to their normal schedule as soon as they can.

Be alert to signs of depression—excessive quietness, fatigue, withdrawal, changes in eating and sleeping patterns, expressions of hopelessness, lack of interest in favorite activities. Encourage adolescents who seem depressed to talk to someone about their feelings—if not you, then another adult they respect and trust, such as a school counselor, a teacher, or a spiritual leader. Don't hesitate to seek professional help if you think or even suspect that it may be needed.

KELLI'S STORY

Kelli was in the eighth grade when her mother died of AIDS, leaving Kelli with her father and older sister. Kelli reacted to her mother's death with anger. "There can't be a God," she often told her friends. "He would never have let this happen. With so many evil people in the world, why did my mother have to die? It's not fair."

In high school, Kelli sought out female teachers and counselors to talk with about her mother's death. She often wrote essays with violent and self-destructive themes. She denied any wish to hurt herself and explained that the essays were just her way of letting her anger out.

One of Kelli's counselors told her about a support group for teens who had lost a parent to AIDS. The group leader, a trained therapist, focused on helping the teens recognize their anger and find appropriate ways of dealing with it, both internally and externally. Kelli attended the group, but she still had problems. She ran away from home twice and was finally placed in a foster home.

Kelli found security and stability in the foster home. She continued going to group and made progress in her ability to get along with others and function in school.

For Kelli, as for many young people who lose a parent, the death of her mother turned her life upside down. She was afraid to face her teen years without her mother. Her fear turned into anger as she realized that her mother was gone forever. Before she could go on with her life, she had to confront both her anger and her fear and recognize the relationship between them. The support group and the foster home gave her the help she needed.

❦

General guidelines for helping children understand death

AS MUCH AS WE'D LIKE to protect children from learning about death, it's up to us—as parents and caring adults—to help them understand this basic reality. In developmentally appropriate ways, we need to assist them in sorting out their emotions and resolving their fears. We need to provide them with coping skills based on rational thinking, laying the groundwork for healthy grieving if and when someone they know dies.

Following are some general guidelines to keep in mind as you work to help your children understand death and accept it as a fact of life.

Be aware of what your children are thinking and feeling

Take time to observe your children in many different circumstances—playing, performing various tasks, interacting with others, or just sitting quietly, engaged with a book or a toy. Listen as they talk to you, as they talk with their friends, and even as they talk or sing to themselves. In this way, you'll develop a good sense of what your children are thinking and feeling. How do they seem to you? How do they sound? What are their worries, their fears, their anxieties? Does death, or the fear of death, come up in their play or their conversations?

It's not necessary to tutor children daily on death and death-related issues. Wait for times when talking about death seems normal, natural, and as comfortable as possible for everyone concerned. Avoid projecting your own fears and anxieties onto your children. Instead, be sensitive to their moods and concerns.

Take advantage of opportunities to talk about death

The death of a pet is a perfect opportunity to introduce children to the concept of death. Although your first response may be to protect them—for example, by flushing the goldfish away—take advantage of this chance to explore a serious subject. Talk with your children about how the goldfish was born into life, lived by eating and breathing, and finally died. Say that the fish has *totally* stopped living and will not come back. Tell them that it is okay to feel sad because the fish died. Explain that feelings of sadness are normal and natural—steps on the road to feeling happy again—and that the sadness will eventually go away. Emphasize that it is *much* better to talk about sadness and feel sadness than to hold it in and pretend it isn't there. Sadness helps to heal the hurt; keeping the sadness inside makes the hurt last longer.

This gentle, matter-of-fact approach is far more effective and memorable than a "lecture" on death, which usually has little meaning or relevance to children. When we "walk" children through an understanding of death, we give them the tools they need to cope with the inevitability of more death in the future.

Be patient

The concept of death is complex and will be difficult for young children to understand. Adolescents who are coming to terms with their own mortality may have a hard time grasping what death is all about. It will probably take many quiet, serious, compassionate conversations with your children to help them understand death. Be willing to take the time it needs.

Be factual

When explaining death to your children, use simple, straightforward language. This will avoid creating fears and misconceptions. Answer their questions with facts and accuracy. Ask them questions in turn to make sure they understand what you are saying.

Be a family

Include all members of your family in discussions about death. In this way, your family will become a support group, sharing information, concerns, and ideas. While individual family members will understand and react to death somewhat differently, depending on their age and stage of development, everyone should have an equal chance for expression, attention, and support. Learn about death as a family—and be sure to explain that talking about death won't *cause* death. Emphasize this point until even young children understand and accept it.

Grieving

THE WORD "GRIEF" comes from the Latin *gravare*, "to burden or make heavy." In grief, all of us must carry a heavy load—the burden of sadness. The ability to carry this load, gradually lessen it, and eventually discard it is the essence of healthy, normal grieving. For children, the loss of a parent or sibling is the heaviest load of all.

It is always difficult to watch children grieve, especially when their behavior seems self-delusional or painful. Feeling the pain and working through the tough initial period is essential to growth and healing. Your first instinct as a parent is to protect your children from pain and distress. But there is a time to reach out, and a time to let go.

There is no single formula for guiding children through grief. Just as children perceive and react to death differently based on their developmental level, experience, knowledge, and environment, they grieve in dramatically different ways. It is important to have a general understanding of how children experience grief at various ages and stages, and that is the subject of this chapter. But before you can help your children, you must first help yourself.

Taking care of yourself

A DEATH IN THE FAMILY affects everyone, including you. Immediately following the death, you may feel fatigued and confused, unable to make decisions or to care for anyone else. This is not abnormal or selfish; it is a natural human response. The death of a loved one can cause mental shock that is just as debilitating as physical shock.

If you have lost a partner, a parent, a sibling, or a child, you are carrying your own heavy load of grief. Meanwhile, your children need you. How can you help them? By regaining as much balance and control over your life as you can, as soon as you can.

Following are several suggestions for you to try. Start with one you think you can manage, then go on to others. You don't have to do them in any particular order. Gradually integrate them into your own grieving process. They won't "cure" your grief, but they *will* make it easier to cope with your grief, and they *will* put you in a better emotional and physical position to help your family during the crisis.

Put major life decisions on hold

A death in the family will bring about changes, but until you regain complete control, keep them to a minimum. This is not the time to sell the house, move, or change jobs, unless you absolutely must. It is not the time to give away the personal possessions of the loved one who has died, or to send the children to live with someone else temporarily.

Wait to make major life decisions until you and your family have settled into a normal functioning mode, when you are thinking clearly. For now, those decisions can wait.

Stay busy

A common initial reaction to the death of a loved one is to become immobilized. Some people take to their beds for days; others do nothing but sit and cry for hours. If you are immobilized, you can't give your children the support they need. Meanwhile, you send them the message that a death brings normal family functioning to a halt, perhaps forever.

Young children lack a strong sense of time. Long periods of inaction with no interaction can be frightening and distressing for them. Force yourself to participate in making arrangements, assisting in family chores, calling friends and relatives, and trying to do some work. Force yourself to *move*.

Take care of your body

Grief can be profoundly exhausting. It's important to keep up your strength with a healthful diet, sufficient rest, and regular, moderate exercise. Be well groomed; you'll feel better about yourself. As an extra precaution, you may want to schedule a checkup with your physician.

Avoid alcohol and other drugs

In our society, the practice of numbing pain is condoned and often encouraged. Well-meaning physicians may prescribe tranquilizers to "help you through." You may feel that a few drinks will ease your pain and help you to function better.

In reality, alcohol and other drugs will blur and interfere with your ability to assume an effective role in your family. You may do or say things that cause harm and create more pain. If, for example, you feel very angry because of the death, the use of alcohol may trigger rage. You should also be aware that alcohol and tranquilizers are depressants. If you are already feeling sad, they will make you more sad and discouraged.

Resume your normal routine

Try to resume your normal routine as soon as possible, as much as you can. You may have to push yourself to return to work, perform normal family functions (prepare meals, shop, pay bills, help the children with their homework), but this is what you need to do.

Getting back to normal enables you to break free of some of the debilitating effects of the mental shock you are experiencing. It also demonstrates to your children that life *does* go on after a death, and that you are healthy and functional and will not abandon them. Resuming your normal routine lessens the chaos within and around you and replaces hopelessness with purpose.

Let your grief show

Playing the hero or heroine following a death doesn't help anyone. Denying your feelings by putting on a brave front sends your children a false message while prolonging and intensifying your own grief. It's okay to cry in front of a child and explain why you are crying and how you are feeling. Expressions of grief are normal; stoic pretense is not.

Young children are confused by stoic behavior. They might wonder, "Why does Mommy seem normal when I feel so sad?" "Doesn't Daddy care what happened?" "If I cry, that will only upset Mom, so I'd better not cry." Children are much more perceptive than we generally give them credit for. They know how we feel and can see beneath the mask. Sharing your grief lessens the burden for everyone.

Help others

When you help others during your time of grief—whether by lending a hand with tasks or providing emotional support—you have less time for self-pity and self-doubt. Meanwhile, you display strength to your children and show that you are beginning to regain control of your life.

Spend time with other adults

Some families react to death by closing ranks and excluding outsiders. You need to spend time with other adults, particularly friends who are not family members. This keeps you in touch with normal life, provides you with comfort and support, and gives you opportunities to voice your concerns and discuss your plans for the future. Friends can provide objective guidance and advice when we are not thinking clearly. And if your friends want to help you, let them.

Keep a journal

This simple technique can go a long way toward helping you work through your thoughts and feelings. Let the words flow; don't edit your writing or worry about grammar or spelling. Write about the events surrounding the death; write about your sadness, confusion, and anger; write about your fears for the future; write about the kindnesses of friends and family members . . . it's *your* journal, so write whatever you choose. You'll find that writing has a cathartic quality. As the words flow from your mind onto paper, some of your pain and grief will follow.

Set limits

Reacting to the pain and stress caused by the death, your children may be angry, destructive, irritable, and rebellious. Although you need to be patient and understanding, you also need to set limits. Point out the connection between their behavior and the death, explain that it's normal for people to react strongly to death, then remind them that certain behaviors are still inappropriate. Make your expectations clear.

You also may need to be patient, understanding—and firm—with your adult relatives and friends. Needy and intrusive family members may create additional stress within your family. Well-meaning friends may hover. Have the courage to ask for privacy and time alone.

Do things that make you feel good

Make time to pursue activities and interests you enjoyed before the death. If you love to garden, spend an hour or two planting seeds or pulling weeds. Read a book, go to a movie, take a walk, pursue a hobby—whatever used to comfort you and promote good feelings. These pleasant experiences will refresh you, strengthen your coping skills, and speed your return to normal functioning.

How children grieve

D URING THE PAST 15 YEARS, we have learned a great deal about children and grief from researchers including Elisabeth Kübler-Ross, John Bowlby, Maria Nagy, and Gerald Koocher. The field experiences of Maria Trozzi of The Good Grief Program and others like her have yielded valuable insights into how children grieve. Still, each child grieves differently, depending on his or her environment, experiences, and developmental level. Each child must be treated as a unique individual in need of compassion and support during a trying time.

The following sections describe in general terms how children of various ages go about grieving. Each section includes suggestions for what you can do and say to help a child through the grieving process. Keep in mind that a child's grief will take many twists and turns, based in part on how well the child comprehends what has happened. Other factors that affect a child's reaction to a death are:

- how the person died

- how the child learned about the death

- the child's relationship or closeness to the deceased

- family relationships and dynamics prior to the death

- the family structure after the death

- how and whether the child's needs are met during the rituals (wake, funeral, burial) following the death.

If the person who died was the child's primary caregiver—the person the child depended on completely—then the grief response will be much more intense than if the deceased did not figure prominently in meeting the child's daily needs. While this may seem obvious, a family immersed in crisis may not be aware of this distinction. It is easy to misunderstand the grief reactions of a child, especially when you are carrying your own burden of grief.

Infants ages newborn to 10 months

It is hard to assess how much infants grieve. What we do know is that they react with distress to the loss of the primary caregiver (usually the mother). In addition, they may be able to sense the distress of those around them when it takes the form of crying, changes in schedules and routines, and additional noise and stimuli in the home environment. The absence of smiling faces, periods of play, and being held may have a cumulative effect. Infants may become cranky, cry often for no apparent reason, and alter their eating and/or sleeping patterns.

❧   WHAT YOU CAN DO   ❧

If the mother becomes terminally ill, it may be best to introduce a surrogate as soon as possible to ease the shock caused by the mother's sudden withdrawal from the infant's world. Perhaps there is an aunt, grandmother, or adult cousin who is willing and able to spend time with the infant frequently and regularly. Or you might find a home-based day-care setting where there are few children and an understanding adult who will devote extra time and attention to the infant.

After a death, try to keep the infant's schedule as close to normal as you can. If the person who died was a parent or sibling—someone the infant saw every day—you may want to arrange for someone else to care for the infant for a short time immediately following the death, providing continuous nurturing in a calm environment.

Children should be told about the death of a parent as soon as they can comprehend it. This usually happens around preschool age, when they start to wonder why they don't have a daddy or a mommy like their playmates or classmates do. They will want to know—they deserve to know—the truth, and they should learn it from a close family member.

Babies ages 10 months to 2 years

As babies become aware that something significant has happened in their world and someone important to them is missing, they may respond with temper tantrums and outbursts of anger—as ways to express their despair and frustration, and as attempts to "bring back" the deceased. They may believe that if Mommy always came to quiet them when they cried, then crying will make Mommy reappear.

Some babies may search for the lost loved one for a period of time—looking around expectantly when Mommy enters the room without Daddy, or watching Daddy's chair as if they expect to see him there—but they will eventually abandon the search. They may show little interest in toys, activities, and food during this period. In addition, they may revert to thumb sucking, curling up in a fetal position, or other infantile behaviors as ways to cope with their distress.

✿   WHAT YOU CAN DO AND SAY   ✿

The best way to support babies through the family's grieving period is to get everyone involved in offering extra love and support. Hold the children often and comfort them. Spend as much time with them as you can.

Children toward the upper end of this age range may express concern about the sadness they see around them. Gently explain that a sad thing has happened. Say that people will feel sad for a time, but they will feel better after a while.

Don't be concerned if children ask the same questions over and over. In many cases, they are just practicing using the language—still a new skill for them, and one they enjoy trying out. All you really need to do is acknowledge their awareness of sadness. You might even reflect their words back to them. In response to "Daddy is sad," say "Yes, Daddy is sad." Sometimes that confirmation is all they need.

Although children in this age group are not able to grasp and articulate everything they are seeing and feeling, they may hold memories of this period into later life. When they are older and better able to comprehend death, you can ask them to share their memories. This will help to facilitate discussion, understanding, and healing.

Children ages 2 to 5

A common misconception is that children in this age group are "too young to understand." In fact, although their understanding doesn't approach that of an adult or an older child, two-to-five-year-olds *do* grieve, feel loss, and experience other strong emotions following the death of a loved one. Because they may respond in puzzling ways, it is sometimes difficult to understand their level of comprehension and their ability to grieve and mourn.

Following are some typical responses that children this age have to death.

Bewilderment
Children might seem totally confused about or disbelieving of what has happened. They may repeatedly ask, "Where is Daddy?" They will want to know when the deceased is going to return, or they may actively look for him or her.

Regression
Many young children revert to regressive behavior—clinging, whining, wetting, asking for a baby's bottle, thumb sucking. Regressive behavior seems to be a way of seeking care and nurturing at a time when they are feeling anxious.

Ambivalence

Some children appear to be completely unaffected by death. They might respond to the news with inappropriate questions or statements—"Can we go to the park today?" "I can't find my doll." Although this is disconcerting, it isn't uncommon. It doesn't mean that the children have accepted or coped with the death, nor does it mean that they don't understand what has happened.

Expressing grief through play

Children who do not openly display their sadness or sense of loss often will reveal it through play. Themes of family loss and death may surface as they play with dolls or action figures, or as they act out home or school roles with friends; for example, they might "lose" a parent figure doll or talk about a family member who is "gone."

This type of play is healthy in that it gives children a comfortable way to express their sadness, anxiety, and distress. It helps them to sort out these feelings and understand them. Children this age may not be capable of expressing their feelings verbally. Their play reflects their yearning for the deceased and signals that they are mourning his or her absence.

Modeling

Many children model the behavior of their parents or other close adult caregivers. A parent who presents a "stiff upper lip" after a death to protect children from sadness may cause them to place their emotions on hold. A parent who shows rage, extreme distress, or hysterical behavior may see this response reflected in his or her children. Because children don't know how to express grief, they will look to older family members for some indication of how to do this.

Separation anxiety

Separation anxiety is a common reaction to traumatic loss among children this age. Subconsciously, they worry that other loved ones will leave them, too. They wonder what will happen to them and how they will survive.

Forming attachments

When a parent dies, young children may form attachments to other adults who resemble or possess qualities similar to the deceased. For example, a girl who has lost her mother might focus on her teacher. Therapists who work with children often note that those who have lost a parent start calling them "Daddy" or "Mommy" or asking them to be their parent. Although this behavior may seem abnormal, it's quite common and may even be beneficial. It does *not* mean that you are failing to meet your children's needs.

Testing reality

Children this age are still sorting out and testing reality. When told about a death in the family, they may initially appear to know and accept what has happened. Then, in the weeks or months that follow, they may ask when the loved one is coming back, or look through the house for him or her. This is not a cause for particular concern. Rather, it is a normal developmental pattern of trying to assimilate what is real and what is not real.

❧   WHAT YOU CAN DO AND SAY   ❧

The first thing you must do for children this age is tell them about the death. Take them aside, go to a quiet place, and speak to them one-on-one. This shows your support and concern for their emotional well-being.

In the case of a prolonged terminal illness, tell children in advance what is going to happen. This gradually eases them into accepting and understanding the outcome of the illness. Keeping the impending death a secret until it happens makes them feel betrayed. Letting them know about it ahead of time gives them the opportunity to learn about death, talk about it, ask questions, and interact with the terminally ill person in ways that will bring long-lasting and consoling memories. Following the death of a parent, the surviving parent should assume the roles and tasks of the deceased parent so the change in the children's routines will be less traumatic.

When talking about death with children this age, use language that is sensitive but direct. It's okay to say "Daddy died" and follow with a clear and careful explanation of what death is. Tell the children that death is permanent. When someone dies, the body loses its ability to eat, sleep, and breathe. It *totally* stops. Speak in a calm, reassuring, matter-of-fact voice about what has happened and what is going to happen next. This will help children to feel more secure about the future.

Remember that children this age are very literal. Here's what *not* to tell them and why:

- *"Daddy has gone to sleep and won't wake up."* Children given this explanation will hold on to the concept of death as temporary. They may believe that Daddy will probably wake up sometime. They may become fearful that the surviving parent will go to sleep and not wake up. They may wonder, "What if *I* fall asleep and don't wake up?" This explanation may lead to sleep disorders as children resist going to bed or falling asleep.

- *"God wanted Mommy and took her to heaven."* Children may think, "What if God wants Daddy? What if God wants *me*?" Their fears and anxieties might increase.

- *"We lost Daddy."* Children may wonder, "What if *I* get lost and can't find my way back home?" Imagine how worried they might become if they are temporarily lost in a supermarket or shopping mall. Children given this explanation may develop separation anxiety and cling to the surviving parent, refusing to leave his or her side and needing to know where he or she is at all times.

- *"Your brother has gone away."* Children may think, "Where has he gone, and why?" They may feel anxious about the future: "What if someone else I love goes away?" This explanation is vague and worrisome to children. It creates more questions than answers.

While there is no such thing as a "perfect script" for this time of crisis, the following will give you a general idea of how to tell a two-to-five-year-old about death:

"Bobby, as you know, Daddy has been very, very, very, very sick for a long time. His sickness has now made Daddy die. This is a sad time for me, and it is a sad time for you, too. Daddy's body has stopped living—he can't breathe, eat, or sleep anymore. He will not be with us because he has stopped living.

"We will miss Daddy, and for a while we will cry and feel sad. It is okay if you cry and want to ask questions. I will be here to take care of you and love you as always. We will still live together as a family. I will not go away from you.

"There will be a lot of people coming to say good-bye to Daddy and to help us as we say good-bye. These people are our family and friends who are trying to help us feel better. They may feel sad and cry, too. We will have a place for people to come to speak with us. We will also go to church to pray and say good-bye.

"After that, Daddy's body will be placed in the ground. He will not be cold or feel anything because all of his feeling has gone from his body. We will put flowers where he has been placed, as part of our good-bye. We will also have Daddy's name on the place. We will visit the place to pray and remember the good times that we had with Daddy.

"After a while, we will all feel better, and the sadness inside of us will go away. We will keep thinking of Daddy, and our thoughts will be happy ones of when he was with us. We will miss him and still love him, but he will not be with us anymore."

You may want to include specific religious or cultural beliefs, if you feel that the child will understand them and they won't further confuse or frighten the child. The telling does not have to be done all at once. As you talk to the child, it may help to hold him or her in your arms. Your touch and physical warmth will provide a sense of security and create trust.

Be patient as children explore and experience grief. Reassure them often that it is okay to cry and feel sad or upset. Share your own feelings, and don't be afraid to cry in front of them.

You will need to be exceptionally patient with children who regress into immature behaviors. Explain that you understand how they feel, but their behaviors are not helpful and only make things harder for everyone. Avoid getting angry or making the children feel guilty. When they behave appropriately, reinforce this with increased warmth and affection. Ignore inappropriate behaviors unless they become truly unmanageable. Use time-outs to give children a chance to calm down and think about their actions.

Provide opportunities for children to act out and talk through their feelings, including play settings and dolls or action figures. Once they are able to express their feelings openly and realistically, they'll be on their way to normal childhood growth and development.

Recall that children in this age group are egocentric by nature. Their primary needs are to survive and to be cared for by others. They have a very strong fear of abandonment. Offer frequent reassurances that you will care for them and be there for them, as you always have.

Don't send the children away. Many families feel that it's best to have their children live with someone else for a period just prior to a death and afterward, during the wake, funeral, home visits, and burial. But the children will know that a death has occurred. Like you, they need to be close to the family and share in the family's grief. Children who are sent away may feel abandoned and confused about why they are being excluded. The physical move to a new and less familiar setting only adds to the stress they already feel. As they grow older, they may resent being deprived of the chance to be with the family and to say good-bye to the deceased.

Finally, avoid excluding and isolating children. Don't send them to their rooms when friends and relatives stop by to offer condolences. Include them in family activities as much as possible. Hold them, hug them, reassure them, and tell them you love them. Although you will be bearing your own load of grief, worry, and stress, be sure to make time for your children. If they understand what is happening and want to attend the funeral and burial, let them. Tell them exactly what will happen and why, and encourage questions.

❧

Children can think that a death is their fault

The death of a loved one—especially a parent—can be so traumatic and bewildering that children resort to "magical thinking." They start to believe that their words and actions have tremendous powers. They remember a time when they yelled "I hate you!" to the parent who has since died. Or they recall a tantrum or other incident of disruptive behavior that made the parent angry or distressed. They wonder if their words or actions actually caused the death.

Be alert to signs of magical thinking and quick to reassure children that the death was not their fault—they had nothing to do with it and couldn't possibly have caused it. For example, if a child says, "I wish I was nicer to Mommy because then she wouldn't be dead," tell the child calmly but firmly that he or she was not responsible for Mommy's death. Explain what really happened, using clear and factual language. Meanwhile, don't be overly concerned; this type of thinking is normal among children in this age group. Your explanations will go a long way toward easing and eliminating their fears.

❧

SELENA'S STORY

Selena was four years old when her father became terminally ill with brain cancer. He spent several long periods in hospitals and then moved to a hospice setting. For the last two months of his life, he returned home, where his wife Cassie and hospice workers cared for him.

Selena was a quiet, bright child who was attending kindergarten at the time of her father's death. Cassie was an open, caring mother who told Selena and her eight-year-old brother Jamal what was happening to their father. She explained that Daddy was very sick and would not get better.

Selena saw her father losing strength and life daily within the home. She showed little emotion and was not interested in speaking about illness or death. Some adults felt that Selena didn't understand what was happening and was "too young" to express her grief.

Meanwhile, Cassie offered her support and talked both of her children through all of the phases of death in the final months. She enlisted the help of a school counselor who was trained in assisting children with grief. During the counseling sessions, Selena chose to play games and talk about school rather than the impending death. Gradually, as trust was built, she listened more attentively to the counselor's guidance, but she still did not speak of death with the counselor, her teacher, or her friends.

Then, about a month before her father died, Selena's class had a voluntary show-and-tell activity. Selena, who normally avoided the limelight of show-and-tell, raised her hand to speak. She walked to the front of the room and said simply, "My father is dying." Her classmates showed little reaction, but her teacher gave her a hug and later related to Cassie and the school counselor what had happened.

Selena had accepted the death, understood it, and gained the courage to express it. By making her announcement, she had actually told *herself* that she was okay.

When her father died, Selena attended the funeral and burial. Soon after, she was able to speak fondly about her memories of her father and function as a normal, healthy five-year-old.

Selena's story emphasizes the importance of not assuming that a child is "too young" to understand or be included in the grieving process. Instead of isolating her or trying to protect her, the adults in Selena's life offered her love and support, people to talk to, and the factual knowledge she needed to handle the crisis. She spoke about her father's impending death when the time was right for her.

❧

MARK'S STORY

Mark came to his new school as a five-year-old kindergartner. He was well dressed, frequently laughed and smiled, was very bright and articulate, and instantly became popular with his classmates. However, he often behaved in ways that were troubling to his teacher and his peers.

Shortly before Mark started kindergarten, his mother was murdered. His parents had separated when Mark was two, and he had seen his father infrequently over the past three years. His mother's death was a nightmare for him. No one explained what had happened. Police detectives questioned him. A social worker took him to his paternal grandmother's house in another city, and that was where he now lived. Mark had not even met his grandmother until he arrived at her door.

At school, Mark often introduced himself by saying, "My name is Mark, and I don't have a mother." At other times he simply blurted, "My mommy was killed." Both his teacher and the school counselor were concerned because Mark refused to speak of his mother's death except in short bursts and exclamations. Mark also had difficulty paying attention in class. He often spoke of fantasy friends and tended to project the roles of mother and father onto other adults around him.

Several factors contributed to Mark's inability to cope and grieve appropriately. First, he was never given the opportunity to grieve. After suffering a major trauma, he was brought by a stranger to another stranger's home and left there. No one told him what would happen in the future. There was no family structure in place to provide him with continuity and ensure his well-being and survival. Mark had no choice but to numb his feelings and retreat into denial.

Fortunately for Mark, his grandmother proved to be very loving and caring. She sought and received help for Mark, who began seeing a child therapist. A social worker provided ongoing support, and the school program met Mark's academic and social needs. In addition, Mark's father reentered his life and began taking a more active parenting role. Still, it seemed likely that Mark's recovery would be long and difficult, and that some of the scars from this tragic episode would remain with him throughout his life.

❧

AMANDA'S STORY

Amanda's father died of a heart attack at the age of 36. Amanda was four years old at the time and in preschool. Her father had a history of heart disease and had been hospitalized several times; death at any moment was a distinct possibility during the last few years of his life. Amanda's mother and father explained his illness in a way that Amanda could understand, and they used the opportunities of seeing dead birds or other animals to point out the reality of death in a comprehensible manner.

When her father died, Amanda seemed relatively unaffected during the initial phase. She didn't cry or want to talk about the loss of her father. Her mother, Jane, perceived her response as the child's inability to grasp the concept of death, and she assumed that Amanda was taking it well.

About a month after the death, however, Amanda started to "feel sick" in the morning and asked to stay home from school. Soon this escalated to refusing to go to school with no pretense of being sick. She clung to Jane, always keeping her in view. At night, before she went to bed, she asked where Jane would be, and often she awoke and climbed into bed with her mother. Amanda continually inquired about Jane's health, repeating the same questions over and over despite reassurances that her mother was fine and would not become sick and die. Whenever Jane came down with a minor illness, such as a cold or the flu, Amanda became very anxious.

Most children who exhibit these behaviors respond well to frequent reassurances of the surviving parent's well-being, along with frank and open conversations about the death and the circumstances that caused it. When they don't respond, therapy can help to bring their fears out into the open and eventually put them to rest. A therapist can also suggest behavior modification techniques. Doing nothing may lead to greater fears and insecurities as the child grows.

❧

Children ages 6 to 9

When children in this age group are told about a death, they usually are able to understand it fully. Unlike their younger siblings, who see death as temporary and unreal, six-to-nine-year-olds know that it is permanent and real. However, they may not be able to comprehend what the death means to their life, and this may become a source of turmoil for them.

Following are some typical responses that children this age have to death.

Denial

A common response among children in the middle years is to deny that the death ever happened. They can be very aggressive in their refusal to accept the death. Some children seem happier and more playful after learning about the death of a loved one, as if they are utterly unaffected by the loss. Adults often misinterpret this as proof that the children are cold or uncaring, or that they never really loved the deceased. The adults may react with anger or simply ignore the children.

In fact, denial indicates the presence of a lot of hurt—so much that children try to build a wall to keep it out. The happier they are and the harder they play, the farther away the pain seems to go. Children in denial need opportunities to grieve, and they may need permission to grieve. Adults give permission when they encourage children to talk about the deceased and their feelings about the loss, and when they themselves model the feelings and behaviors of grieving.

Idealization

Sometimes children this age respond to death by idealizing the deceased. They may insist that "my mom was the smartest woman in the world" or "my dad was the strongest man in the world" or "my sister was perfect." This allows them to maintain a fantasy relationship with the person who has died.

Guilt

Among six-to-nine-year-olds, guilt is a common response to death, especially if they are unable to express their sadness about the loss. If the deceased ever made casual statements like "You'll be the death of me," children may think that their misbehavior contributed to or even caused the death.

If they are also in denial, and if they put on a brave act as part of their denial, their guilt might be compounded by adults who correct them or get angry with them for not appearing to care about the death. Children who are in denial and overwhelmed with guilt will have difficulty resolving these issues without help.

Fear and vulnerability

Children in this age group understandably react to death with fear and vulnerability. They want to hide these feelings, especially from their peers, because they don't want to appear "different" from their friends and classmates. Boys in particular may act tough or aggressive.

If a parent has died, children may fear for the survival of the remaining parent. They may be reluctant to leave the parent's side, worry about his or her health, and refuse to attend school. Like two-to-five-year-olds, they experience separation anxiety.

Caretaking

Six-to-nine-year-olds who are grieving the death of a parent may assume the role of the deceased mother or father. They might suddenly become the caretaker of younger siblings, or take on chores that were previously performed by the deceased parent.

Searching for the person who has died

In the weeks and months following a death, children will often search for the person who has died. This behavior is not exclusive to children. People of all ages tend to search for the deceased. While young children might go from room to room or look in the attic or basement, adults have reported scanning the faces in a crowd or staring at the driveway as if expecting the loved one to appear. Even in the animal kingdom, birds and mammals have been known to search for a dead mate for a period after the death.

❧ WHAT YOU CAN DO AND SAY ❧

Tell the children about the death as soon as possible, following the same general guidelines suggested for children ages two to five. Give them as much information as you think they can comprehend. If the death was anticipated—if the person who died was very ill—you might say, "Daddy had a very, very, very, very serious disease. It got worse, but now it has stopped, and Daddy's body is no longer alive."

Let the children know how you feel, and allow them to react as they wish. Encourage them to speak about the death. Children who have lost a loved one often feel powerless and helpless; talking about death in a safe, supportive setting with someone who cares is important to their recovery.

Children in denial need to be comforted and given permission to grieve. You might say something like this: "You don't have to show your sadness to everyone, but it's okay to share it with me or other family members. If you want to cry and feel sad in private, that's okay, too, but after a private sad time, it would be good to talk with someone about how you feel."

Be alert to signs that children are idealizing the deceased. Encourage them to talk about the loved one as he or she really was—a human being who wasn't perfect and who sometimes made mistakes, just like the rest of us.

Searching for the deceased may seem delusional and self-destructive, but it is a normal response to such a severe loss. Children in this age group know that they will not really find the person alive (as do older children and adults who engage in this behavior), but the physical and emotional acts of searching help them break through the shock of grief and come to terms with the fact that the loved one is indeed gone. The best response is simply to let them search. Comfort them by explaining that you, too, feel like searching at times. Explain that searching is one way to get through the tough part of accepting what has happened. Offer reassurances that their pain and loneliness will gradually lessen and they will start to feel better.

This is an extremely trying time for everyone, and emotions are very near the surface. Children might say or do things that seem inappropriate. It's perfectly all right to correct them, but do so with an extra measure of love and support. Tell them that when people feel sad, confused, or afraid, they sometimes act in ways they wouldn't usually act. Be sure to respond *appropriately* to inappropriate behaviors, and separate the behavior from the child. For example, you might say, "Hitting your sister is not allowed, so you need a time-out. When your time-out is over, you can apologize to her." Be matter-of-fact and avoid suggesting that the child should feel guilty or remorseful.

Children in this age group may grieve in spurts. They may seem fine and well adjusted for weeks or months, then enter a period of crying, yearning, and clinging. Often these periods of grief will coincide with birthdays, holidays, or other occasions—the anniversary of the death, a family vacation—that evoke memories of the deceased. Try to anticipate these times. Talk with the children in advance to prepare them, let them know what to expect, and give them the opportunity to share their feelings.

❦

Art can help children
work through their grief

Children love art. They love to draw, as drawing allows them to express their feelings without fear of criticism or the need to interact with others. Parents and teachers should encourage children who have lost a loved one to draw pictures of how they feel, of times they spent with the deceased, of the rituals and events following the death, or anything they wish to express about the loved one or the death.

Dr. Elisabeth Kübler-Ross has written extensively about the therapeutic effects of drawing for children who are grieving. Drawing gives them a way to let their feelings flow onto paper. When no one tells them how or what to draw, drawing becomes cathartic. Children should be free to choose whether to share and discuss their drawings with others or keep them private.

Depending on how the children feel, the subject matter of their drawings may vary widely. Don't be alarmed by representations of caskets, burials, or the deceased. What's important is to give children a way to release their feelings at a time of inner turmoil. Let their expression flow as a means of healing.

❦

KATHY'S STORY

Kathy was six years old and about to enter first grade when her mother died of breast cancer. Although Kathy knew her mother was very sick, she never acknowledged the possibility of her death. During the six months before her mother died, Kathy's aunt took care of her before and after school because her father worked long hours. At night, however, Kathy went to her mother's room to hear her mother read to her.

Kathy's two older siblings (ages eight and ten) did not visit their mother much. The seriousness of her illness caused them too much pain and worry. They stayed away as an act of denial.

When told of her mother's death, Kathy cried and grieved openly, while her other siblings withdrew to themselves. After the funeral, she often asked her father or aunt to bring her to her mother's grave. She wondered out loud if her visits to her mother's room at night had "made her too tired" and had somehow "made her die." She felt guilty for having wanted her mother to read to her.

The loss of a mother is traumatic for all children, but it is particularly devastating to young girls, since the mother is their role model for growing up. Fortunately for Kathy, she had a female surrogate in her aunt, who was able to spend time with her regularly. Her aunt reassured her that she had not been responsible for her mother's death in any way, and that her mother had looked forward to Kathy's nightly visits. She encouraged Kathy to remember the good feeling of being with her mother and hearing her read. Kathy took comfort from her aunt's words and presence, and eventually accepted that she had not caused her mother's death.

❧

MIGUEL'S STORY

Miguel was a nine-year-old third grader when his father died of cancer. He had visited his father daily in the hospital prior to the death. He had seen his father grow thin and lose his hair, and he had noticed his father's skin discoloration and pain. Miguel asked his mother many questions, and she gently informed him that his father would not recover. When his father died, Miguel was taken to visit the body. He was allowed to attend the wake, funeral, and burial.

Miguel's attitude and behavior became very mature in the weeks and months following his father's death. He began taking care of his three-year-old sister. He didn't cry, explaining that he had to "be strong" for his mother. In school, his behavior was good, although he was more quiet than he had been before his father died.

A school counselor had been working with the family through the period of crisis. Several months after the death, the counselor spoke with Miguel to see how he was doing. Miguel told the counselor that he accepted the death but missed his dad. He frequently visited his father's room and smelled his aftershave because it brought back happy memories. He also spent time looking at things his father had given to him (books, baseball cards) and thinking about occasions when they had played together. Miguel still insisted that he had to "be strong" for his mother. He worried that she might become sick and die, leaving him and his sister with no parents.

Miguel loved to draw, and he often drew pictures of churches. He always included a casket somewhere in the drawing. When the counselor asked Miguel to tell why the casket was there, Miguel explained that it helped him to remember his father and how he had looked the last time Miguel saw him.

Miguel did not appear to be troubled by this memory. Drawing caskets was a means of grieving and resolving his sadness. When the counselor asked Miguel if he ever cried, the child said, "Sometimes . . . when I'm alone."

It was clear to the counselor—and to Miguel's mother—that the boy was coping well with his grief. Knowing in advance that his father would die gave him a gradual road to understanding what was happening in his world. He had the support of adults who took his questions seriously and answered them honestly. Miguel missed his father, but he was going to be all right.

♥

Preadolescents ages 10 to 12

Preadolescence is a transitional period, full of complexities, challenges, and confusion. Children are moving away from being totally dependent on others and starting to explore their independence. Some are eager to make the change; others don't want to leave childhood and are disconcerted by the early signs of puberty. Yet they all feel the need to develop their own identity.

As the winds of change swirl around them, preadolescents seek care and comfort from their peers. Children in this age group put a high value on group status. To wear the "right" clothes with the "right" brand names, speak the "right" language, and listen to the "right" music are required for acceptance into the group. Being "different"—too tall, too short, too thin, too heavy, too smart, too slow—is to fall into disfavor with the group.

The death of a loved one, especially a parent, is often perceived as something that brands them as "different." They fear that expressing their grief might be seen as a sign of weakness. Boys in particular may refuse to cry or show emotion, as this makes them appear vulnerable. They bury their feelings, even the deep sadness that follows a death.

Children may hold off any outward signs of grief, trying to remain above the emotional pain. As a result, they may seem unmoved, apathetic, or uncaring. Their pain is present, however, and it will emerge at some point. Often, their delayed grief surfaces well after the rest of the family has moved on to living normally again.

When preadolescents show their grief, it can take many forms. Like six-to-nine-year-olds, they might start caretaking—assuming the role of the deceased, "parenting" younger siblings, and acting more adult. Or they might display anger in ways that are uncharacteristic for them—being aggressive, bullying, rebelling, being irritable. Taking their point of view, they have good reason to be angry. They have been cheated out of a loved one's guidance, affection, and support. They have been made to appear "different" within their group. Their future plans and hopes have been interrupted.

Fear is another factor among preadolescents after the loss of a loved one. Fear of their own mortality, of losing the other parent, of being abandoned as they move into adolescence, of the unknown—all are possible reactions to a death. Their fear may be expressed as physical complaints, moodiness, sleep difficulties, eating problems, and a lack of interest in attending school.

Some preadolescents attempt to create a "bond" with their deceased parent by collecting photos of him or her, spending time in the parent's old room, taking on similar mannerisms, or wearing clothing, perfume, or aftershave that reminds them of the loved one they have lost. These behaviors are normal, healthy expressions of sadness and yearning. They enable the children to feel closer to the deceased and hold on to pleasant memories.

❧   WHAT YOU CAN DO AND SAY   ❧

Many of the suggestions mentioned earlier for helping children ages six to nine are also effective with preadolescents. Give them time to talk, ask questions, and express their grief. Share your feelings with them.

For preadolescents who seem fearful, take special care to acknowledge their grief and address their fears. For those who are angry, be patient with their inability or unwillingness to express grief at appropriate times and in appropriate ways. Continue to offer your love, understanding, and support. Arrange to speak with them privately, then explain how fear, worry, anger, frustration, and pain are all normal feelings at a time of crisis and loss. Invite them to tell you how they feel. You might ask them to write about their feelings or make a list of things they are worried about. Guarantee confidentiality—anything said between you stays between you—and offer information as needed. Tell them that adults also feel fear, worry, anger, frustration, and pain when a loved one dies.

Avoid making statements like "If your father were alive, he would want you to make the honor roll" or "Now you're the man (or the woman) of the house." This puts additional pressure on preadolescents at a time when pressure is the last thing they need. Give them room to mourn and yearn for the deceased.

Encourage them to spend time with their peers in the weeks and months following the death. They should know that it's okay to go to dances or parties, go out with their friends, or have friends over. Because group interaction among preadolescents is vital to normal growth, they need to maintain their social ties.

Perhaps most importantly, let them know daily that you are there for them. Tell them that you are doing everything in your power to get things back to normal so they can resume their lives.

❧

Writing can be a way to say good-bye

Some children who are grieving the loss of a loved one may prefer to write about their emotions. Encourage them to keep a journal, write letters to their friends, write poems, or create a prayer or eulogy.

If the death was sudden and unexpected, you might suggest that children write a letter to the deceased. One of the most painful aspects of sudden death is that it deprives children (and adults, for that matter) of the chance to say good-bye. Writing a letter gives children the opportunity to feel closer to the loved one who has died, to express their feelings of sadness and yearning, to remember shared experiences and happy times, and finally to say good-bye. This is not morbid. It is healing.

A letter to the deceased may be kept secret, placed at the grave, burned in the fireplace, or shared and discussed within the family, perhaps as part of a private memorial service. The choice should always be the child's.

❧

LUKE'S STORY

Luke's mother, a single parent, was afraid for her 12-year-old son. In recent months, Luke had become involved with a gang. He had abandoned his old friends and started to hang out with a group of teenagers in a park known for violence and drugs. He refused to obey curfew, his grades slipped dramatically, and his attitude was sullen and unresponsive. His mother sought help from a therapist.

At first, Luke attributed his behavior changes to "growing up." He wouldn't acknowledge that he belonged to a gang, but he alluded to secret names and signs that indicated his involvement. "I like my friends at the park," he said. "I belong, and they like me." When asked to describe his family, Luke told of the deaths of his grandfather, uncle, and aunt. All three had died during the last four years as the result of violence.

When asked to talk more about the deaths, Luke replied that his grandfather's death bothered him the most. After three years, he still felt sad about it. He would not allow himself to cry, however. Nor would he admit to being worried or upset about the high incidence of violent death in his family.

Luke's attachment to a gang was his response to the basic need for security in the face of trauma and grief. He believed that the older boys would protect him, accept him, and offer him safe passage as he entered adolescence. Death—the antithesis of youth and life—had been thrust upon him. He feared for his own mortality, and he perceived the gang as providing him with the safety he needed to survive.

❧

STEPHEN'S STORY

Stephen was 11 years old when his father, a firefighter, suffered a fatal heart attack at work. The sudden loss shook Stephen's whole life. He had lost more than a parent; he had also lost his best friend. During the past few years, he and his father had spent a great deal of time together. They went camping on his father's days off, and his dad always attended his Little League games. The two had grown very close. Now Stephen's father had been snatched away.

Meanwhile, Stephen's mother was having difficulty adjusting to the death of her husband. She often asked her son, "How could your father leave me? What am I going to do?" These questions increased Stephen's fear and distress. He lay awake at night, worrying about what would happen to him and his mother in the future.

Stephen attended his father's wake and funeral, and he found some comfort in the number of firefighters and police officers who came to pay tribute. Few of his peers attended, however, and those who did said little to him. Stephen felt numb. He was remotely aware that he should have felt *something* and perhaps even cried, as many others did. Instead, he stood expressionless and silent.

Six months passed before Stephen was able to talk about his father and how much he missed him. During the interim, his mother had made gradual adjustments and was better at dealing with her own loss, but she was concerned about Stephen's delayed grief reaction. She encouraged him to rejoin his peer group and let him know that she was available to listen.

When his closest friends also offered their support, Stephen was finally able to release his emotions. Although his pain and sorrow were great, he allowed himself to grieve.

❧

Adolescents

Adolescent grief has an intensity all its own. Adolescents are already in a tumultuous state of change; life is just beginning for them, and death is a shock to their basic life system. Especially when a parent dies, the shock takes the form of repression and disbelief.

Most boys will not allow themselves to cry, especially in the presence of their peers. Girls are more likely to show their emotions and seek comfort and support from family members and friends. Teens tend to band together in times of crisis, but the death of a loved one may create too much emotional turmoil to share. Adolescents may feel that shutting down their emotions is the best way to weather the storm.

Many teens are somewhat cynical or depressed about life in general. A death can magnify those feelings. This can lead to acting out, fighting, poor school work, alcohol or other drug use, and inappropriate or unhealthy relationships. On the other hand, teens who have a clear understanding of death as part of the life process, and who may have had past experience with grief, are able to express their grief in normal, productive, appropriate ways. They are able to talk about it, cry, and give and receive support.

Many adolescents become caretakers for their families after a death. This gives them a way to feel productive rather than useless during the shock period. They usually care for their younger siblings, but they might also offer support to adults.

Guilt takes on a new dimension in the teen years. As part of the "breaking away" period, teens frequently clash with their parents over issues involving independence, privacy, rights, etc. These teen-parent conflicts—present in every family with teenagers—can come back as guilty memories when a loved one dies. They may be too painful to talk about, and some teens might conclude that the conflicts somehow contributed to the death.

❧   WHAT YOU CAN DO AND SAY   ❧

Give adolescents the chance to spend time with their friends in the period following the death. The peer support system prevalent among teens will comfort them during this distressing time. Many adolescents benefit from attending support groups, where they are able to express their feelings with others who share common bonds of experience and age.

Provide structure and guidance, even if your efforts meet with resistance. Adolescents want and need this structure to avoid getting involved in situations that will only cause them (and you) greater distress.

Try to maintain family closeness, with adolescents playing important roles in carrying out responsibilities and helping younger siblings. This helps to assuage any feelings of guilt and brings about a greater sense of security within the family and within the teens themselves.

Don't hesitate to tell adolescents that it's okay to cry, that you love them and will be there for them, and that time will gradually heal their pain and insecurity about the future.

JULIA'S STORY

Julia was a 14-year-old eighth grader when she suddenly began to exhibit periods of giddiness followed by crying in school. Until then, she had been quiet and reserved. Two of Julia's friends told the school counselor about her behavior change.

The counselor called Julia to her office to try to learn the reason for her unusual behavior. Julia told the counselor that one of her closest friends, an eighth grader at another school, had died two days earlier following a severe asthma attack. Julia, who lived with her father, had no one to talk to about her friend's death. Her father would not allow her to go to the wake or the funeral, which were scheduled for the next two days. Julia was very distraught that she would not be able to be with her friend's family or say good-bye to her friend.

The counselor invited Julia to talk about her friend, including both her pleasant memories and her present shock at the death. She encouraged Julia to realize that she had been a good friend to the girl and had made her life happier when they were together. Julia poured out her grief and thoughts about death. Together, she and the counselor scheduled a series of follow-up sessions to monitor Julia's progress as she grieved.

Meanwhile, the counselor called Julia's father and asked him to consider letting Julia attend the wake and funeral. The counselor explained that it was very important for Julia to be there. The father agreed, and Julia went to both services.

During her next session with the counselor, Julia reported that her friend's family had hugged her and asked that she sit near them. She was already resolving much of her pain and anxiety over the loss of her friend.

❦

ELLEN'S STORY

Ellen was a 16-year-old high school junior when her father committed suicide. Her father had been an alcoholic, and Ellen's mother had left him two years earlier, taking Ellen to live with her.

Both Ellen and her mother had a very hard time dealing with the father's suicide. They felt guilty and responsible. They wondered if things would have turned out differently if the family had stayed together. Maybe then the father wouldn't have killed himself. Maybe he killed himself *because* they had left him.

For several days after her father's death, Ellen cried at school. She became totally withdrawn and uninterested in her school work. When she was referred to the school counselor, she refused to talk about the death, insisting that it wasn't a school issue.

Ellen's friends rallied around her. Gradually she started telling them about her grief and feelings of guilt. The counselor stayed in touch and recognized the changes Ellen was going through. She referred Ellen to a young female therapist at another site.

Ellen started attending weekly therapy sessions that focused on helping her to let go of her guilt. Meanwhile, she and her mother began attending a support group for suicide survivors, where they learned that guilt is a common reaction to suicide. They gained comfort and solace from knowing they were not alone.

At school, Ellen remained somewhat withdrawn, but she was able to function and even extended her circle of friends.

❧

General guidelines for helping children work through grief

PERMANENCE, ETERNITY, FOREVER—these are difficult concepts for anyone to grasp. The sorrow we feel when a loved one dies is not for the deceased, but for ourselves. We know that our loss is permanent and that it will affect us for the rest of our lives. The fact that we will *never* again see or speak with someone we love is the core of the pain we feel. Accepting this fact is essential to healthy grieving.

Children of all ages mourn and yearn for loved ones who die. There is no map we can use to mark milestones in their grieving process. However, we do know that grief is best managed when it is out in the open, and that children cope better with loss in a safe, caring, warm environment that promotes and encourages the expression of emotions. Providing this environment at a time of deepest distress is an act of love. It lets children know that you understand, you care, and you want to help them through this difficult period.

There is no magic formula that tells us how long children will grieve. However, some factors do seem to have an effect.

- Was the death anticipated or sudden? (Generally speaking, grief lasts longer in cases of sudden death.)

- How close was the child to the deceased? (The closer the relationship, the longer the grief period.)

- How well does the child comprehend what dying means? (Children who understand death seem to move more smoothly through grief than children who are struggling with the concept.)

- How much support can the family give? (The more support, the better.)

- Will the child be allowed and encouraged to mourn? (This promotes normal, healthy grieving.)

Chronic grief—an intense grief that starts at the time of the death and lasts for long periods—is rare.

The path that a child will follow through grief is as unpredictable as children themselves. The best we grownups can do is to be alert for various signs and stages—shock, denial, disbelief, fear, guilt, anxiety, and acceptance—then offer the right words at the right time. Even when children don't show any outward signs of grief, they may still be grieving. Sometimes we need to give permission for grief to be a private and personal matter.

As you help your children through the process of grieving, you may find the following guidelines useful.

Give them your time

The period surrounding a death is often chaotic and frenzied; time may become a blur. The well-being of your children should be a top priority. The grief children feel is intense, and they require comfort and care to get through it. They need opportunities to ask questions, express their feelings, and experience the presence of caring adults.

Set aside a specific time each day for one-on-one interaction with your children. Let them know when "their" time will be, and adhere to it faithfully. Take them to the park, go for a walk, play a board game, or watch a video. You don't have to talk about the death or the deceased; all you have to do is be together.

Your special attention shows love and support at a time when your children need it the most. Continue this practice daily for as long as possible, since it will promote healing and growth for months after the death.

Be there for them

As your children cry, get angry, or feel guilty or remorseful about the death, be there for them. Holding their hand, holding them in your lap, or hugging them are all ways to share your strength and offer reassurance. Sit quietly with them while they cry, and don't hold back your own tears if they come. Prove by example that crying is okay.

Your close physical presence provides great comfort and security. It lets your children know that you are there to ease them through this difficult time.

Let others help

Following a death, friends and family may offer to help out with tasks and responsibilities. Let them! This allows you to conserve your energy and strength. It gives you more time to work through your grief—and more time to spend with your children.

Let go

Let go of preconceived notions of how children "should" grieve. Each child is a unique individual; each grieves in his or her own way. Let your children experience and express their emotions however they choose.

Avoid saying "You have to be brave" or "Don't cry in front of everyone" or "You're the man in the family now." These types of messages suppress and delay children's grief and mourning. Their anger, pain, guilt, and sorrow *will* come out eventually; trying to stop them only postpones the inevitable. Meanwhile, the feelings intensify.

Give them opportunities for expression

Children may not be prepared or equipped to express their feelings in a meaningful way. The emotions that follow the trauma of a death may be entirely new to them, and they may not have the words to describe them. Try giving them other ways to express themselves. Encourage them to draw, paint, write letters, take photographs, make collages, write songs, write poems . . . whatever they choose. Invite them to share their work with you, if they want to share it.

Keep them physically active

The death of a loved one can deplete our strength and leave us feeling exhausted and depressed—literally "held down" by trauma. We slow down mentally and physically. Our thoughts and actions are subdued as negative energy saps our emotions. The tendency is to give up and give in to the feeling of depression. We eat less, sleep less, and move less.

Offer grieving children many opportunities for physical activity, and encourage them to participate. Going back to the soccer, softball, or baseball team, taking up martial arts, dance, or gymnastics, even walking the dog—all are healthy ways to combat depression. Breaking the inertia caused by the trauma of death is one of the first steps a child can take toward recovery.

The Chinese use the word *ch'i* to describe the life force. Each day, millions of Chinese people practice set routines of movements that they feel enhance the flow of their *ch'i*. Westerners are only beginning to acknowledge the existence of the mind/body connection. The relationship between mental and physical health is slowly being explored, accepted—and respected.

Read a book together

There are many books available for children that provide information about grief and grieving. Reading a book can be therapeutic. Some children prefer to read in private, but most children love it when their parents read to them. Don't pass up this opportunity for closeness. Sit next to your children, hold them on your lap, or pull up a chair beside their bed and read. If they truly want to read a book about grief on their own, ask if you can borrow it when they're through. Read it yourself, then ask if they want to discuss it.

On pages 94–95, you'll find a list of books that are useful for easing the pain of loss and promoting healthy grieving.

Find a support group

Children often interact better with other children than they do with adults. Many mental health clinics, hospitals, and social service agencies sponsor support groups for children who have suffered the loss of a family member. The groups give children the chance to hear and speak with others who are experiencing feelings similar to theirs. Children learn that they are not alone, they are not "different," and it's okay to talk about what they are going through.

When telling children about a support group, present it as a positive opportunity to learn, grow, and be with other people their age who know how they feel. Tell them that a support group is not a place for children who are "crazy" or "sick." If they enjoy school, you might try saying that a support group is like a class, but without tests or grades. Explain that they will learn many things that will help them now and in the future.

Know when to seek professional help

The grieving process may last up to a year or longer. Most children weather it reasonably well, with periods of normal behavior interrupted by spurts of grief. However, some children have great difficulty with grieving. Be alert for the following:

- excessive and prolonged periods of crying

- frequent and prolonged temper tantrums

- extreme changes in behavior

- noticeable changes in school performance and grades

- withdrawal for long periods of time

- lack of interest in friends and activities they used to enjoy

- frequent nightmares and sleep disturbances

- frequent headaches and/or other physical complaints

- weight loss

- apathy, numbness, and a general lack of interest in life

- prolonged negative thinking about the future, or lack of interest in the future.

Seek help for children who display these attitudes or behaviors. They can indicate the presence of depression or unresolved grief.

Commemoration

DURING THE GRIEVING process, there comes a time to bring emotions into perspective, modify patterns of thinking, develop a new awareness of the loss and the importance of life, and start to free oneself from the burden of grief. This change—and it is a significant one—is facilitated by the act of commemoration.

While they are grieving, children are focused on their own feelings. Shock, denial, regression, guilt, and yearning are all self-directed emotions. This is not to say that children are selfish or egocentric; *all* people react to death according to how it affects them personally. This is natural and healthy. To release the grief, to recognize and sort out the maze of emotions and move toward acceptance of the loved one's death, are part of the healing process.

A child once told me that she had seen a rainbow near the beach where she and her deceased brother had played. She said that the rainbow was his way of letting her know that everything was okay and she should stop worrying about him.

We all need rainbows when a loved one dies. We all need to rest, rejuvenate ourselves, and go on with our lives, whether we are six years old or sixty. Commemoration is the act of simultaneously looking back and looking ahead.

To commemorate the life of someone we loved is to celebrate that life and give thanks for the parts we shared.

Too often, we try to avoid memories of loved ones who have died, or we refuse to speak of them. We try to keep troubling feelings—pain, sadness, yearning—from surfacing again. But commemoration is a positive act. It directs troubling feelings outward and allows healing emotions to be directed inward. It empowers us to rid our minds of turmoil by giving something back to the deceased. When you and your children commemorate someone who has died, you are showing that guilt, anger, and remorse are ending their hold on your family. The focus is now on the good of the past and the promise of the future.

Once the initial, immobilizing shock of a death has diminished, children usually welcome the opportunity to commemorate. It enables them to say and do the things necessary to ease their mind and allow the joy of childhood back into their life. Real sadness comes from believing that the memories of the loved one have been buried with the body. To most people, these memories are dear, and preserving them is important.

Generally speaking, children are ready to commemorate a loved one about six months after the death. Of course, there are times when commemoration is appropriate much sooner—or later. Each situation is unique.

Suggestions for commemorating a loved one

A T AN ELEMENTARY SCHOOL where I work, there was an elderly woman who volunteered in the classrooms for many years. She read to the children, cleaned their faces after lunch, bandaged skinned knees, and gave hugs when needed. Then, within a few short days, she became ill and died. Everyone who knew her was shocked and saddened by this sudden loss.

The school and the children chose to commemorate their friend for the kindness and love she had given them. The children wrote letters, made drawings, and created posters and other art displays to honor her. A celebration with her family was held in the school library, where cake and cookies were served and a plaque was placed to keep her memory alive. This act of commemoration helped the children to resolve their grief, look back with joy, and move ahead enriched by the experience.

Commemoration can take many forms—public or private, simple or lavish, short-term or perpetual. Following are several suggestions to share with your family. Read through them, talk about them, and decide which ones you want to try. Make sure that your children have an equal voice. Choose one or more to do as a family, then tell your children that they can also commemorate the loved one in their own ways. Explain that their goal is to bring back fond memories. Whatever they do will be right for them, because commemoration is a personal matter.

Display photographs

Place family pictures or portraits of the deceased throughout the home, especially in the children's rooms. Give some photographs of the loved one to your children, and explain that these are *their* special pictures to keep in a safe place and look at whenever they choose. Sometimes all pictures of the deceased are taken down or hidden away in an attempt to avoid painful memories. In fact, removing these literal representations implies that all relationships with the loved one are over and should be banished from our thoughts. This sudden emptiness is more painful than the sight of a beloved face. Photographs enrich our memories and make it easier to move from loss, through grief, to acceptance.

Make a photo album

Invite your children to help you gather photographs of the deceased and place them in an album. Reminisce about what was happening when each picture was taken. The stories will have special meaning for your children and will rekindle fond memories whenever they page through the album.

Visit the grave

Visits to the grave should be relaxed and pleasant, not occasions for searching or sadness. Tell your children that the purpose is to remember happy times and celebrate the loved one's life.

You may find it comforting and healing to speak your thoughts to the loved one during these visits. Explain to your children that talking to the deceased is a way of saying the things you wanted to say while he or she was alive but didn't have the chance. Make sure they understand that this is not a magical way of "contacting" the person. Rather, it's a way of comforting ourselves by voicing our thoughts.

Write a poem

Encourage your children to write a poem dedicated to the loved one who has died. Frame their poems and display them in a prominent place to view as the years go by. Children love poetry and often find comfort in this form of expression, which honors the memory of the deceased. You might also keep the poems in a small book to be cherished and shared.

Plant a tree

The tree represents a new life and a living tribute to the deceased. Whenever your children see "Daddy's tree," it will bring back fond memories of the times they spent with him. As your children grow and become strong, so will the tree. Let them know the reason for planting the tree, and point out how you feel when you look at it.

Make a charitable donation

There is comfort in giving to others in memory of a deceased loved one. His or her name is written or spoken often and associated with benevolence and goodwill. A charitable donation symbolizes the positive aspects of the person's life and keeps them in the present for family members and others who were touched by that life.

Remember the loved one on holidays

Holidays and anniversaries are difficult for families and children who have suffered a loss. "The first Christmas without Mommy," "the first birthday without Dad," "the day my brother died"—all can give rise to new spurts of grief.

You might invite your children to incorporate some kind of commemoration into these special days. A plant or flower arrangement bearing the loved one's name, a prayer or poem read aloud at the dinner table in the person's honor, an evening spent telling stories about the deceased—any of these can make you and your children feel closer to your loved one during trying times. Some families publish remembrances in the local newspaper on holidays or anniversaries, a public statement that they still cherish the memory of one who has died.

Establish a commemorative tradition for the community

Create a scholarship fund at your children's school, give a trophy to a Little League or softball team, start an award program for community service, maintain a flower bed in your neighborhood or city . . . these are all uplifting, lasting ways to commemorate the deceased. People are touched by such giving and will join in the commemoration as they participate in the ceremonies. Your children will take pride and comfort in the fact that the loved one's memory is kept alive in this positive and generous way.

ANDRE'S STORY

Andre was a 14-year-old eighth grader when his grandfather died suddenly of a stroke. Andre had always been very close to his grandfather. He responded to the death with the normal shock, fear, and confusion we all feel at such times. He attended the wake and funeral, and he returned to school a week after his grandfather was buried.

At school, he seemed quiet and calm. He appeared to accept his grandfather's death but did not want to talk about it. He wanted to get things back to normal as quickly as possible, even though his life had changed dramatically.

Six months passed, during which Andre never discussed his grandfather's death or showed any signs of grief or sadness. Finally he was referred to a therapist for counseling. When the therapist asked him to talk about his feelings related to his grandfather's death, Andre simply shrugged. "I'm doing okay in school," he said. "Why should I talk about my feelings? I don't see the point."

Then the therapist asked, "Are you sorry that you didn't have the chance to say good-bye?"

Andre responded with a rush of emotions. As his repressed feelings surfaced, he admitted that he was haunted by the fact that he hadn't been able to speak with his grandfather right before he died. He hadn't "made peace" with him or said good-bye. Andre revealed a concern he had never told anyone: "Maybe if I had been there, I could have saved him."

Often, in cases of sudden death, older children feel that they were cheated out of the opportunity to say good-bye. Teenagers especially may harbor guilt for "transgressions" against the deceased with no chance of ever making amends. They may need help resolving these issues and finding closure.

It would have been best for Andre if he had said good-bye at the wake and funeral, and if he had talked about his grandfather's death soon after it happened. Since those options no longer existed, the therapist suggested that Andre say good-bye in other ways. Perhaps he could write a letter to his grandfather, or visit his grave and speak his thoughts there. The choice was Andre's.

❧

ROSA'S STORY

Rosa was away at college when her mother died of cancer. The two of them had been very close for many years; Rosa's father was also alive, but he was almost 15 years older than her mother. During the first part of Rosa's freshman year, her mother often visited her at college. Her disease had progressed to the point where she couldn't climb the stairs to Rosa's third-floor dormitory room. Rosa was always upset after these visits. Each time, she saw how her mother's condition had worsened.

Rosa also felt guilty about being away from her mother. She often told her friends, "I'm missing her last days. How can I stay here? I should be home with her." Her mother, however, insisted that she remain at school. Every weekend, Rosa drove an hour and a half each way to see her parents. Shortly after Christmas, her mother died.

Rosa cried often at first and felt a great loss. She bonded closely with the other young women in her dormitory, who provided her with compassion and offered her the opportunity to express her grief openly. For a time, she feared losing her father because of his age (67), but she was able to focus on the fact that he was in good health and still very active.

Rosa worked hard at school to earn good grades as a tribute to her mother. She often told her friends that she felt her mother was watching over her, and she wanted to make her proud. She and her father planted a tree in their backyard as a memorial for her mother, and they grew closer in their shared grief. Rosa eventually graduated with honors.

Healing and acceptance

C OMMEMORATION IS A VITAL PART of healing and recovery. It promotes acceptance of the loss and helps survivors overcome their pain, fear, and loneliness. It fosters serenity.

In 1934, a man named Reinhold Niebuhr wrote a prayer that is very appropriate at any stage of grieving and healing. You may want to share it and discuss it with your children:

> *God, grant us the serenity to accept the things we cannot change,*
> *Courage to change the things we can,*
> *And wisdom to know the difference.*

Looking back at a loved one's life with fond remembrance, and marking that life in meaningful ways, shows that we are finding the peace that comes with acceptance. We know that we cannot bring the person back to life. The fact of the death cannot be changed. There is no longer any room for guilt, remorse, or regret. Instead, we are filled with love and quiet solace.

This is what you want for your children. Encourage them to find comfort by commemorating the loved one who has died.

Moving on with life

HELPING YOUR CHILDREN to recover from the death of a loved one takes caring, commitment, and time. The trauma children experience as a result of the loss erodes their self-esteem and sense of security. The future, as they see it, is clouded with doubt. They may believe that the death has made them "different" from their peers, and that they will always be burdened by grief and guilt.

Recovering from a death does not mean erasing all sadness, yearning, and distress. It is not a form of selective amnesia, where the death of the loved one is forgotten. The deceased was, and should always remain, an important part of the children's lives. This is one purpose of commemoration. But children should be encouraged to move on with their life, set and attain goals, play and socialize with their peers. Eventually they will come to accept the death as a reality, accept the changes it brings, and make the internal adjustments needed to progress as normal, healthy, happy human beings.

General guidelines for helping children move on with life

HOW LONG CAN IT TAKE for children to recover from the loss of a loved one? The old saying, "Time heals all wounds," does not apply here. Time helps to dull the intensity of the pain, and memories fade with time, but the passage of time alone is not a healer.

There is no formula that tells us how long it will take a child to return to normal after a death. Some researchers believe that it takes up to two years for the intense pain to diminish. How close the child was to the loved one, the age of the child, and the circumstances of the death all play a role in determining the length of time a child will need.

Following are some guidelines to keep in mind as you help your children toward recovery.

Be patient but firm

Be patient as children cry, get angry, ask questions, and express their insecurity and frustration. (You might also ask them to be patient with *you* during this trying time.) Don't ask children to "be brave" or to "remember that Mommy would want you to be grown-up now." Give them time and space to explore their feelings and still be children.

Being patient doesn't mean allowing inappropriate behavior. Children need limits, especially when their emotions are in turmoil and their lives have been turned upside down by a loved one's death. If they act out, avoid responsibility, or refuse to do their school work, they need to know that these behaviors are not acceptable. If they express their feelings in inappropriate or destructive ways, they need to be shown better ways to express them. Be clear with your children about what you expect from them. Regardless of how rebellious they may seem, they really do want limits and structure in their lives.

Some parents tend to be overly indulgent and forgiving of children after a death because of "what the children have been through." This is a mistake. Let your children know that you still expect them to do their chores, finish their homework, and behave appropriately. Follow through with consequences when they break the rules. You are not being "too hard" on your children. You are showing your love and concern for them, and you are giving them a sense of security.

Promote positive self-esteem

Do whatever you can to boost your children's self-esteem at a time when it has been badly shaken. Praise and compliment them at every opportunity. Show genuine interest in their school work, interests, outside activities, and friends. Listen when they talk, and give them as much individual attention as you can. Spend time with them at night to comfort them and ease them to sleep. Be generous with hugs and kind words. Display your love openly and smile at them a lot. Tell them how proud you are of them. Now more than ever, your children need to know how important they are to you.

Provide encouragement and direction

The loss of a loved one may leave children with a feeling of despair—that nothing matters, there is very little they can control, and the future is uncertain and unpredictable. They may withdraw into inaction as a way to protect themselves.

Encourage your children to play, to participate in activities they enjoy, and to spend time with friends. Give them opportunities to enjoy life and go back to being children. Help them to focus on the present—and the future. Tell them about changes that will take place because of the death, but put them in positive terms.

Work with your children to set reachable goals. At first, these can be simple, short-term goals. Gradually, as their recovery progresses, the goals can be more complex and long-term.

For young children who appear worried and anxious, it may help to make detailed daily schedules. Specify when they will get up in the morning, when they will be picked up from school, what they will do after school, what they will have for dinner, and when they will go to bed. This will provide a sense of security and give them specific events to look forward to and count on. Gradually cut back on scheduling as the children develop their own routines and rejoin the mainstream. Older children will benefit from discussions of high school and college plans.

By focusing on the future, you signal to your children that the past cannot be changed and it's time to move on with their lives. Remind them often that their pain will lessen and that the future holds promise for them.

Give choices

Letting children make choices empowers them and gives them a sense of control over their lives. In one-on-one discussions or family meetings, provide your children with options. Within reasonable limits, let them decide when to do their homework and chores, what after-school programs to participate in, what library books to read, and so on. Invite them to help you plan family vacations and outings, and include them in family decisions.

Teach problem-solving skills

Problem-solving skills are useful in all areas of life. Teaching your children problem-solving skills helps to reduce anxiety and promote self-esteem. When children know how to approach a problem and work through it on their own, they feel more confident about the future.

One simple way to teach problem-solving skills is by presenting children with hypothetical dilemmas, then having them brainstorm and evaluate possible solutions. For example:

> "Your best friend has been buying you candy, toys, and other presents. One day he says that he wants to tell you a secret, but you have to promise not to tell anyone else. You promise. Then your friend tells you how he has been paying for your presents. He has been taking money out of his mother's purse a little at a time. What will you do?"

Write each proposed solution at the top of a sheet of paper. Below the solution, draw two columns. Head one column "Pluses" and the other "Minuses." Have children evaluate each solution by listing its pluses and minuses. Encourage them to come up with other solutions and analyze those as well.

Stick together

Let your children know that you are still a family. Explain that a family working together to overcome grief and move on with life is stronger than individuals trying to do it on their own. Sadness is more bearable when it is shared; memories are more precious when they are held in common; planning for the future is more exciting when everyone gets involved. As long as you're a family, no one is alone.

Give them permission to be happy again

Children who are mourning a loss need permission to be happy again. They need to know it's okay to play, learn, laugh, and love. Just as children model the behavior of adult caregivers during the grieving process, they will want to know how to act during recovery. Set a good example. Spend time with friends, share jokes, relax, smile, and go back to enjoying life. Tell your children that a happy, successful life can be the best way to commemorate someone who has died. That is what the loved one would have wanted.

Finding help

COPING WITH THE LOSS of a loved one is one of the most difficult challenges you and your children will ever face. Seeking help, support, and comfort, gaining knowledge, and finding peace are essential to recovery. Following are lists of organizations to contact and books to read for more information and assistance along the way.

Organizations

Centering Corporation
P.O. Box 3367
Omaha, NE 68103
Telephone: (402) 553-1200

The Centering Corporation provides excellent guidance for families experiencing grief. Request a copy of their catalog describing many books, pamphlets, and videos that focus on dealing with grief.

The Compassionate Friends
P.O. Box 3696
Oak Brook, IL 60521
Telephone: (708) 990-0010

The Compassionate Friends is a national network of support groups that focus on assisting parents who have lost a child. Parents can also find advice and support for helping surviving children cope with the loss of a sibling.

The Elisabeth Kübler-Ross Center
South Route 616
Head Waters, VA 24442
Telephone: (703) 396-3441

The Elisabeth Kübler-Ross Center is dedicated to carrying on the work of Dr. Ross. In addition to seminars, retreats, and lectures, the Center offers an assortment of literature based on her work.

The Good Grief Program
Judge Baker Children's Center
295 Longwood Avenue
Boston, MA 02115
Telephone: (617) 232-8390

The Good Grief Program provides guidance and assistance to parents and teachers on all aspects of childhood grief. It is nationally recognized for its outstanding work in this field, and it often serves as a resource in crisis situations. The staff members are caring and dedicated, and they have the most current data available on how to help grieving children.

Grief Education Institute
2422 South Downing
Denver, CO 80210
Telephone: (303) 777-9234

The Grief Education Institute offers telephone counseling, educational materials, and a newsletter.

Recommended reading

Blume, Judy. *Tiger Eyes*. (New York: Dell, 1982.) A boy journeys through grief after his father is shot. For ages 10 and up.

Boulden, Jim, and Joan Boulden. *Saying Good-bye*. (Weaverville, CA: Boulden Publishing, 1992. Toll-free telephone 1-800-238-8433.) This activity book for ages 4–14 won a National Hospice Organization Award. It is recommended for parents and professionals who are helping children deal with grief.

Buscaglia, Leo F. *The Fall of Freddie the Leaf: Story of Life for All Ages*. (Thorofare, NJ: Charles B. Slack, 1982.) As Freddie experiences the changing seasons along with his companion leaves, he learns about the delicate balance between life and death. For ages 3 and up.

De Paola, Tomie. *Nana Upstairs and Nana Downstairs*. (New York: Putnam, 1973.) A classic story about a small boy's relationships with his grandmother and great-grandmother, the power of love, and how a child perceives death.

Fox, Sandra. *Good Grief: Helping Groups of Children Deal with Loss When a Friend Dies*. (Boston: New England Association for the Education of Young Children, 1988.) Specific, helpful information from the founder of The Good Grief Program. To order a copy, call Maria Trozzi's office at (617) 826-0690.

Gootman, Marilyn E. *When a Friend Dies: A Book for Teens About Grieving and Healing*. (Minneapolis: Free Spirit Publishing, 1994.) Gentle advice for grieving teens who are coping with the death of a friend.

Krementz, Jill. *How It Feels When a Parent Dies*. (New York: Knopf, 1988.) This moving and insightful book features the real-life stories of children who have lost a parent. Share it with your children to help them understand that they are not alone and their feelings are not unusual.

Kübler-Ross, Elisabeth. *On Death and Dying.* (New York: Macmillan, 1993.) An acknowledged classic, first published in 1970, this is the definitive work on death and the emotions involved with it. Dr. Kübler-Ross's lifelong pursuit to assist people in bereavement is set forth here in a sensitive, factual, encompassing way.

Neeld, Elizabeth Harper. *Seven Choices: Taking the Steps to New Life after Losing Someone You Love.* (New York: Dell, 1992.) The author describes her own journey through grief following the sudden death of her husband. She points out how the ability to grasp reality and make positive choices is vital to finding your way through the maze of crushing emotions. A beautifully written book.

Simon, Norma. *The Saddest Time.* (Chicago: Albert Whitman Concept Books, 1986.) A read-aloud book and discussion-starter for children ages 5 and up, this book explains death as the inevitable end of life and illustrates three situations in which children experience powerful emotions when someone close has died.

Index

About the author

WILLIAM C. KROEN received his M.Ed. in Counseling Psychology from Boston State College and his Ph.D. from Boston College. A licensed psychotherapist, he has authored many books and articles on parenting and psychology. Since 1971, he has been a teacher, adjustment counselor, and mediation specialist for the Cambridge, Massachusetts, public schools, where he provides counseling and therapy for children in crisis and those with emotional or behavioral problems.

More Free Spirit Books

Make Someone Smile
and 40 More Ways to Be a Peaceful Person
by Judy Lalli, M.S.
Photographs by Douglas L. Mason-Fry
Simple words and warm, appealing black-and-white photographs present clear and understandable ideas for being a peaceful person and promoting peaceful thoughts and behaviors. The photographs feature children of many races modeling the skills of peacemaking and conflict resolution in their everyday lives.
$8.95, 80 pp., B&W photos, s/c, 8 1/4" x 7 1/4", all ages

When a Friend Dies
A Book for Teens about Grieving and Healing
by Marilyn E. Gootman, Ed.D.
Marilyn Gootman offers genuine understanding and gentle advice for any grieving teen. She knows what teenagers go through when another teen dies; she has seen her own children suffer from the death of a friend. She has written this book out of compassion, love, and a genuine desire to help young people cope and heal.
$7.95, 120 pp., s/c, 5" x 7", ages 11 & up

Just Because I Am
A Child's Book of Affirmation
by Lauren Murphy Payne, M.S.W.
illustrations by Claudia Rohling
Warm, simple words and enchanting full-color illustrations strengthen and support children's self-esteem. Ideal for early elementary, preschool, day care, and the home.
$6.95, 32 pp., color illust., s/c, 7 5/8" x 9 1/4", ages 3–8

Leader's Guide
by Lauren Murphy Payne, M.S.W.
and Claudia Rohling
This leader's guide and the child's book provide a complete first course on self-esteem. Includes 19 reproducible handout masters.
$12.95, 56 pp., illust., s/c, 8 1/2" x 11", preschool through grade 3

Fighting Invisible Tigers
A Stress Management Guide for Teens
Revised and Updated Edition
by Earl Hipp
Proven, practical advice for teens on coping with stress, being assertive, building relationships, taking risks, making decisions, dealing with fears, and more. A perennial best-seller.
$10.95, 160 pp., illust., s/c, 6" x 9", ages 11 and up

Leader's Guide
12 Sessions on Stress Management and Lifeskills Development
Revised and Updated Edition
by Connie C. Schmitz, Ph.D.
with Earl Hipp
Twelve independent, flexible sessions teach specific stress-management skills. Includes 24 reproducible handout masters.
$19.95, 136 pp., illust., s/c, 8 1/2" x 11", grades 6–12

The Families Book
True Stories about Real Kids and the People They Live With and Love, Fun Things to Do with Your Family, Making Family Trees and Keeping Family Traditions, Solving Family Problems, Staying Close to Faraway Relatives, and More!
by Arlene Erlbach
Photographs by Stephen J. Carrera
First-person stories, photographs, and how-tos celebrate families in their diversity. As young reader's discover that families come in many shapes, sizes, and types, they learn to appreciate how important families are to everyone.
$12.95, 128 pp., B&W photos, s/c, 6" x 9", ages 9–13

Kids with Courage
True Stories about Young People Making a Difference
by Barbara A. Lewis
Eighteen remarkable kids speak out, fight back, come to the rescue, and stand up for their beliefs, proving that anyone, at any age, can make a difference in the world.
$10.95, 184 pp., B&W photos, s/c, 6" x 9", ages 11 and up

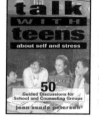

Talk with Teens about Self and Stress
50 Guided Discussions for School and Counseling Groups
by Jean Sunde Peterson, Ph.D.
Fifty guided discussions on success and failure, loneliness, procrastination, test scores, and other topics help students share their feelings and concerns, gain self-awareness and self-esteem, make better decisions, and cope with stress. Includes 20 reproducible handout masters
$19.95, 192 pp., Otabind lay-flat binding, 8 1/2" x 11", grades 7–12

Talk with Teens about Feelings, Family, Relationships, and the Future
50 Guided Discussions for School and Counseling Groups
by Jean Sunde Peterson, Ph.D.
This book presents 50 new guided discussions on topics important to young people today: mood swings, disappointment, anger, change, sadness, depression, conformity, sexual behavior, violence, maturity, gossip, career choices, dating, and more. Includes 26 reproducible handout masters
$21.95, 216 pp., Otabind lay-flat binding, 8 1/2" x 11", grades 7–12

What Kids Need to Succeed
Proven, Practical Ways to Raise Good Kids
by Peter L. Benson, Ph.D., Judy Galbraith, M.A., and Pamela Espeland
Based on a nationwide survey of over 270,000 young people, this groundbreaking book spells out 30 developmental "assets" all kids need to succeed in life and stay out of trouble, then gives more than 500 suggestions for building assets at home, at school, in the community, and in the congregation.
$4.99, 176 pp., s/c, 4 1/8" x 6 7/8", for parents, teachers, community and youth leaders, and teens

Find these books in your favorite bookstore, or write or call:

Free Spirit Publishing Inc.
400 First Avenue North, Suite 616
Minneapolis, MN 55401-1730
Toll-free (800) 735-7323, Local (612) 338-2068
Fax (612) 337-5050
E-mail help4kids@freespirit.com